Literature & Thought

D0797114

ON THE EDGE OF SURVIVAL

Perfection Learning

EDITORIAL DIRECTOR   Julie A. Schumacher

SENIOR EDITOR   Terry Ofner

EDITOR   Sherrie Voss Matthews

PERMISSIONS   Laura Pieper

REVIEWER   Ann L. Tharnish

DESIGN AND PHOTO RESEARCH   William Seabright and Associates, Wilmette, Illinois

COVER PHOTO   FIRE DOWN ON THE LABRADOR 1980 David Blackwood

ACKNOWLEDGMENTS
"Allen Greshner" from *Class Dismissed! High School Poems* by Mel Glenn. Copyright © 1982 by Mel Glenn. Reprinted by permission of the author.
"Appetizer" from *Ghost Traps* by Robert H. Abel. Copyright © 1991 by Robert H. Abel. Reprinted by permission of The University of Georgia Press.
"Battle by the Breadfruit Tree," from *On Safari* by Theodore J. Waldeck, Kurt Wiese, illustrator. Copyright © 1940 by Theodore J. Waldeck, renewed © 1968 by Jo Besse McElveen Waldeck. Used by permission of Viking Penguin, a division of Penguin Putnam Inc.
"Contents of the Dead Man's Pockets" from *The Third Level* by Jack Finney. Reprinted by permission of Don Congdon Associates, Inc. Copyright © 1956 by the Crowell Collier Publishing Co., renewed 1984 by Jack Finney.
CONTINUED ON PAGE 144

Paperback ISBN: 0-7891-5052-2
Cover Craft ® ISBN: 0-7807-9023-5

WHAT CAN BE LEARNED FROM SURVIVAL LITERATURE?

The question above is the *essential question* that you will consider as you read this book. The literature, activities, and organization of the book will lead you to think critically about this question and to develop a deeper understanding of risk-taking and the will to survive.

To help you shape your answer to the broad essential question, you will read and respond to four sections, or clusters. Each cluster addresses a specific question and thinking skill.

CLUSTER ONE Why do people take risks? **HYPOTHESIZE**

CLUSTER TWO After surviving? **GENERALIZE**

CLUSTER THREE What would you risk? **EVALUATE**

CLUSTER FOUR Thinking on your own **SYNTHESIZE**

Notice that the final cluster asks you to think independently about your answer to the essential question — *What can be learned from survival literature?*

AT THE EDGE OF THE GARDEN
1986
Olivia Parker

DONE WITH

My house is torn down—
Plaster sifting, the pillars broken,
Beams jagged, the wall crushed by the bulldozer.
The whole roof has fallen
On the hall and the kitchen
The bedrooms, the parlor.

They are trampling the garden—
My mother's lilac, my father's grapevine,
The freesias, the jonquils, the grasses.
Hot asphalt goes down
Over the torn stems, and hardens.

What will they do in springtime
Those bulbs and stems groping upward
That drown in earth under the paving,
Thick with sap, pale in the dark
As they try the unrolling of green.

May they double themselves
Pushing together up to the sunlight,
May they break through the seal stretched above them
Open and flower and cry we are living.

Ann Stanford

ON THE EDGE
OF SURVIVAL

Table of Contents

"To Fall in the Dark Void"
Lessons of Survival

On July 23, 1988, a man died in a mountain climbing accident in Aspen, Colorado. At the time of his death, Heinz R. Pagels was famous—not as a daredevil, but as a great physicist. He also wrote popular books that made difficult scientific concepts understandable to nonscientists. His ideas even found their way into both the novel and movie of Jurassic Park.

Friends, family, colleagues, and fans grieved Pagels' death. Perhaps some of them felt a touch of unspoken anger as well. Why did such a brilliant and well-loved man repeatedly pursue the dangerous thrills of mountain climbing? Couldn't he have satisfied himself with adventures of the mind?

People who actively court danger are often asked why they do it. The world seems risky enough without pursuing further hazards. Who can say when survival might become an issue? Natural disasters like earthquakes, tornadoes, and floods strike without warning or reason. So do life-threatening illnesses. Much of today's world is plagued by poverty, famine, violent crime, and terrorism. And during the last half-century, the survival of humanity itself has seemed threatened by nuclear war and a ravaged environment. In such a world, why go out and look for risks?

Risk takers often justify their experiences in terms of skill, elegance, and beauty. When asked by a friend why he climbed, Pagels

spoke of the rewards "of sight, of pleasure, of the thrill of pitting my body and my skills against nature." And the American author Ernest Hemingway praised the bullfight as "the only art in which the artist is in danger of death." Perhaps, then, there is something to be gained by risking one's life. "What does not destroy me," wrote the German philosopher Friedrich Nietzsche, "makes me stronger."

But there is a flaw in Nietzsche's reasoning. What doesn't kill us can cripple us in body or mind—or both. People who face dangers through no choice of their own often recall their experiences less happily than deliberate risk seekers. While some survivors feel enriched and strengthened by their experiences, many suffer flashbacks, post-traumatic stress, and even guilt.

This is especially true of those who have experienced the greatest brutalities of the twentieth century. The Italian author Primo Levi endured a year in a Nazi death camp, then wrote powerfully about his experiences in such works as *Survival in Auschwitz*. Millions of readers were moved by Levi's descriptions of Nazi horrors, but even more by his abiding optimism and his faith in human reason. These readers were devastated by Levi's suicide in 1987. In the end, their hero was destroyed by demons that even he couldn't describe.

Survival, then, can be a mixed blessing. So is there any purpose in deliberately putting one's own life in jeopardy? Heinz Pagels offered a poetic answer to critics of his passion for climbing—an answer that speaks of survival as a sublime mystery. At the end of his book *The Cosmic Code*, Pagels described a dream about falling that eerily anticipated his own death. In the dream, his fall from a cliff began with terror, but his feelings quickly changed:

"A feeling of pleasure overcame me. I realized that what I embody, the principle of life, cannot be destroyed. It is written into the cosmic code, the order of the universe. As I continued to fall in the dark void, embraced by the vault of the heavens, I sang to the beauty of the stars and made my peace with the darkness."

CONCEPT VOCABULARY

You will find the following terms and definitions useful as you read and discuss the selections in this book.

credo statement of belief

dehydration extreme depletion of bodily fluids

exposure condition of being unprotected from severe weather and the elements

hubris exaggerated pride or self-confidence

idealism a practice or belief in a standard of perfection, beauty, or excellence; a theory or practice that affirms the value of imagination over reality

idyll a lighthearted, carefree period of life

intimidate to compel or deter by threats or fear

itinerary proposed route of a journey; a travel diary

obsession persistent preoccupation with an idea, feeling, or person

primal primitive

security freedom from danger

self-reliance trusting in one's own efforts or abilities

terrain the physical features of a piece of land

will mental power used to wish a specific outcome

CLUSTER ONE

WHY DO PEOPLE TAKE RISKS?

Thinking Skill   HYPOTHESIZING

WILDING

JANE YOLEN

Zena bounced down the brownstone steps two at a time, her face powdered a light green. It was the latest color and though she didn't think she looked particularly good in it, all the girls were wearing it. Her nails were striped the same hue. She had good nails.

"Zen!" her mother called out the window. "Where are you going? Have you finished your homework?"

"Yes, Mom," Zena said without turning around. "I finished." *Well, almost,* she thought.

"And where are you—"

This time Zena turned. "Out!"

"Out where?"

Ever since Mom had separated from her third pairing, she had been overzealous in her questioning. *Where are you going? What are you doing? Who's going with you?* Zena hated all the questions, hated the old nicknames. *Zen. Princess. Little Bit.*

"Just out."

"Princess, just tell me where. So I won't have to worry."

"We're just going Wilding," Zena said, begrudging each syllable.

"I wish you wouldn't. That's the third time this month. It's not . . . not good. It's dangerous. There have been . . . deaths."

"That's gus, Mom. As in bo-gus. Ganda. As in propaganda. And you know it."

"It was on the news."

Zena made a face but didn't deign to answer. Everyone knew the news was not to be trusted.

"Don't forget your collar, then."

Zena pulled the collar out of her coat pocket and held it up above her head as she went down the last of the steps. She waggled it at the window. *That,* she thought, *should quiet Mom's nagging.* Not that she planned to wear the collar. Collars were for little kids out on their first Wildings. Or for tourist woggers. What did she need with one? She was already sixteen and, as the Pack's song went:

> *Sweet sixteen*
> *Powdered green*
> *Out in the park*
> *Well after dark,*
> *Wilding!*

The torpedo train growled its way uptown and Zena stood, legs wide apart, disdaining the handgrips. *Hangers are for tourist woggers,* she thought, watching as a pair of high-heeled out-of-towners clutched the overhead straps so tightly their hands turned white from blood loss.

The numbers flashed by—72, 85, 96. She bent her knees and straightened just in time for the torp to jar to a stop and disgorge its passengers. The woggers, hand-combing their dye jobs, got off, too. Zena refused to look at them but guessed they were going where she was going—to the Entrance.

Central Park's walls were now seventeen feet high and topped with electronic mesh. There were only two entrances, built when Wilding became legal. The Westside Entrance was for going in. The Fifty-ninth Eastside was for going out.

As she came up the steps into the pearly evening light, Zena blinked. First Church was gleaming white and the incised letters on its facade were the only reminder of its religious past. The banners now hanging from its door proclaimed WILD WOOD CENTRAL, and the fluttering wolf and tiger flags, symbols of extinct mammals, gave a fair indication of the wind. Right now wind meant little to her, but once she was Wilding, she would know every nuance of it.

Zena sniffed the air. Good wind meant good tracking. If she went predator. She smiled in anticipation.

Behind her she could hear the *tip-taps* of wogger high heels. The woggers were giggling, a little scared. *Well,* Zena thought, *they should be a little scared. Wilding is a pure New York sport. No mushy woggers need apply.*

She stepped quickly up the marble steps and entered the mammoth hall.

PRINT HERE, sang out the first display. Zena put her hand on the screen and it read her quickly. She knew she didn't have to worry. Her record was clear—no drugs, no drags. And her mom kept her creddies high enough. Not like some kids who got turned back everywhere, even off the torp trains. And the third time, a dark black line got printed across their palms. A month's worth of indelible ink. *Indelis* meant a month full of no: no vids, no torp trains, no boo-ti-ques for clothes. And no Wilding. *How,* Zena wondered, *could they stand it?*

Nick was waiting by the Wild Wood Central out-door. He was talking to Marnie and a good-looking dark-haired guy who Marnie was leaning against familiarly.

"Whizzard!" Nick called out when he saw Zena, and she almost blushed under the green powder. Just the one word, said with appreciation, but otherwise he didn't blink a lash. Zena liked that about Nick. There was something coolish, something even statue about him. And something dangerous, too, even outside the park, outside of Wilding. It was why they were seeing each other, though even after three months, Zena had never, would never, bring him home to meet her mother.

That dangerousness. Zena had it, too.

She went over and started to apologize for being late, saw the shuttered look in Nick's eyes, and changed her apology into an amusing story about her mom instead. She remembered Nick had once said, *Apologies are for woggers and kids.*

From her leaning position, Marnie introduced the dark-haired guy as Lazlo. He had dark eyes, too, the rims slightly yellow, which gave him a disquieting appearance. He grunted a hello.

Zena nodded. To do more would have been uncoolish.

"Like the mean green," Marnie said. "Looks coolish on you, foolish on me."

"Na-na," Zena answered, which was what she was supposed to answer. And, actually, she did think Marnie looked good in the green.

"Then let's go Wilding," Marnie said, putting on her collar.

Nick sniffed disdainfully, but he turned toward the door.

The four of them walked out through the tunnel, Marnie and Lazlo holding hands, even though Zena knew he was a just-met. She and Marnie knew everything about one another, had since preschool. Still, that was just like Marnie, overeager in everything.

Nick walked along in his low, slow, almost boneless way that made Zena want to sigh out loud, but she didn't. Soundless, she strode along by his side, their shoulders almost—but not quite—touching. The small bit of air between them crackled with a hot intensity.

▲   ▲   ▲

As they passed through the first set of rays, a dull yellow light bathed their faces. Zena felt the first shudder go through her body but she worked to control it. In front of her, Lazlo's whole frame seemed to shake.

"Virg," Nick whispered to her, meaning it was Lazlo's first time out Wilding.

Zena was surprised. "True?" she asked.

"He's from O-Hi," Nick said. Then, almost as an afterthought, added, "My cousin."

"O-Hi?" Zena said, smothering both the surprise in her voice and the desire to giggle. Neither would have been coolish. She hadn't known Nick had any cousins, let alone from O-Hi—the boons, the breads of America. No one left O-Hi except as a tourist. And woggers just didn't look like Lazlo. Nick must have dressed him, must have lent him clothes, must have cut his hair in its fine duo-bop, one side long to the shoulder, one side shaved clean. Zena wondered if Marnie knew Lazlo was from O-Hi. Or if she cared. *Maybe,* Zena thought suddenly, *maybe I don't know Marnie as well as I thought I did.*

They passed the second set of rays; the light was blood red. She felt the beginnings of the change. It was not exactly unpleasant, either. *Something to do,* she remembered from the Wilding brochures she had read back when she was a kid, *with manipulating the basic DNA[1] for a couple of hours.* She'd never really understood that sort of thing. She was suddenly reminded of the first time she'd come to Wild Wood Central, with a bunch of her girlfriends. Not coolish, of course, just giggly girls. None of them had stayed past dark and none had been greatly changed that time. Just a bit of hair, a bit of fang. Only Ginger had gotten a tail. But then she was the only one who'd hit puberty early; it ran in Ginger's family. Zena and her friends had all gone screaming through the park as fast as they could, and they'd all been wearing collars. Collars made the transition back to human easy, needing no effort on their parts, no will.

---

1 **DNA:** acronym for *deoxyribonucleic acid;* cellular compound that carries genetic information.

Zena reached into the pocket of her coat, fingering the leather collar there. She had plenty of will without it. *Plenty of won't, too!* she thought, feeling a bubble of amusement rise inside. *Will/won't. Will/won't.* The sound bumped about in her head.

When they passed the third rays, the deep green ones, which made her green face powder sparkle and spread in a mask, Zena laughed out loud. Green rays always seemed to tickle her. Her laugh was high, uncontrolled. Marnie was laughing as well, chittering almost. The green rays took her that way, too. But the boys both gave deep, dark grunts. Lazlo sounded just like Nick.

The brown rays caught them all in the middle of changing and—too late—Zena thought about the collar again. Marnie was wearing hers, and Lazlo his. When she turned to check on Nick, all she saw was a flash of yellow teeth and yellow eyes. For some reason, that so frightened her, she skittered collarless through the tunnel ahead of them all and was gone, Wilding.

The park was a dark, trembling, mysterious green; a pulsating, moist jungle where leaves large as platters reached out with their bitter, prickly auricles.[2] Monkshood and stagbush, sticklewort and sumac stung Zena's legs as she ran twisting and turning along the pathways, heading toward the open meadow and the fading light, her new tail curled up over her back.

She thought she heard her name being called, but when she turned her head to call back, the only sounds out of her mouth were the pipings and chitterings of a beast. Still, the collar had been in her pocket, and the clothes, molded into monkey skin, remained close enough to her to lend her some human memories. Not as strong as if she had been collared, but strong enough.

She forced herself to stop running, forced herself back to a kind of calm. She could feel her human instincts fighting with her monkey memories. The monkey self—not predator but prey—screamed, *Hide! Run! Hide!* The human self reminded her that it was all a game, all in fun.

She trotted toward the meadow, safe in the knowledge that the creepier animals favored the moist, dark tunnel-like passages under the heavy canopy of leaves.

However, by the time she got to the meadow, scampering the last hundred yards on all fours, the daylight was nearly gone. It was, after

---

2 **auricles:** ear-shaped appendages.

all, past seven. Maybe even close to eight. It was difficult to tell time in the park.

There was one slim whitish tree at the edge on the meadow. Birch, her human self named it. She climbed it quickly, monkey fingers lending her speed and agility. Near the top, where the tree got bendy, she stopped to scan the meadow. It was aboil with creatures, some partly human, some purely beast. Occasionally one would leap high above the long grass, screeching. It was unclear from the sound whether it was a scream of fear or laughter.

And then she stopped thinking human thoughts at all, surrendering entirely to the Wilding. Smells assaulted her—the sharp tang of leaves, the mustier trunk smell, a sweet larva scent. Her long fingers tore at the bark, uncovering a scramble of beetles. She plucked them up, crammed them into her mouth, tasting the gingery snap of the shells.

A howl beneath the tree made her shiver. She stared down into a black mouth filled with yellow teeth.

"Hunger! Hunger!" howled the mouth.

She scrambled higher up into the tree, which began to shake danger-ously and bend with her weight. Above, a pale, thin moon was rising. She reached one hand up, tried to pluck the moon as if it were a piece of fruit, using her tail for balance. When her finger closed on nothing, she chittered unhappily. By her third attempt she was tired of the game and, seeing no danger lingering at the tree's base, climbed down.

The meadow grass was high, and tickled as she ran. Near her, others were scampering, but none reeked of predator and she moved rapidly alongside them, all heading in one direction—toward the smell of water.

The water was in a murky stream. Reaching it, she bent over and drank directly, lapping and sipping in equal measure. The water was cold and sour with urine. She spit it out and looked up. On the other side of the stream was a small copse of trees.

Trees! sang out her monkey mind.

However, she would not wade through the water. Finding a series of rocks, she jumped eagerly stone-to-stone-to-stone. When she got to the other side, she shook her hands and feet vigorously, then gave her tail a shake as well. She did not like the feel of the water. When she was dry enough, she headed for the trees.

At the foot of one tree was a body, human, but crumpled as if it were a pile of old clothes. Green face paint mixed with blood. She touched the leg, then the shoulder, and whimpered. A name came to her. Marnie?

Then it faded. She touched the unfamiliar face. It was still warm, blood still flowing. Somewhere in the back part of her mind, the human part, she knew she should be doing something. But *what* seemed muddled and far away. She sat by the side of the body, shivering uncontrollably, will-less.

Suddenly there was a deep, low growl behind her and she leaped up, all unthinking, and headed toward the tree. Something caught her tail and pulled. She screamed, high, piercing. And then knifing through her mind, sharp and keen, was a human thought. *Fight.* She turned and kicked out at whatever had hold of her.

All she could see was a dark face with a wide hole for a mouth, and staring blue eyes. Then the creature was on top of her and all her kicking did not seem to be able to stop it at all.

Courtesy: Jane Corkin Gallery, Toronto

The black face was so close she could smell its breath, hot and carnal. With one final human effort, she reached up to scratch the face and was startled because it did not feel at all like flesh. *Mask,* her human mind said, and then all her human senses flooded back. The park was suddenly less close, less alive. Sounds once so clear were muddied. Smells faded. But she knew what to do about her attacker. She ripped the mask from his face.

He blinked his blue eyes in surprise, his pale face splotchy with anger. For a moment he was stunned, watching her change beneath him, no longer a monkey, now a strong girl. A strong, screaming girl. She kicked again, straight up.

This time he was the one to scream.

It was all the screaming, not her kicking, that saved her. Suddenly there were a half-dozen men in camouflage around her. Men—not animals. She could scarcely understand where they'd come from. But they grabbed her attacker and carried him off. Only two of them stayed with her until the ambulance arrived.

▲　▲　▲

"I don't get it," Zena said when at last she could sit up in the hospital bed. She ached everywhere, but she was alive.

"Without your collar," the man by her bedside said, "it's almost impossible to flash back to being human. You'd normally have had to wait out the entire five hours of Wilding. No shortcuts back."

"I know that," Zena said. It came out sharper than she meant, so she added, "I know you, too. You were one of my . . . rescuers."

He nodded. "You were lucky. Usually only the dead flash back that fast."

"So that's what happened to that . . ."

"Her name was Sandra Maharish."

"Oh."

"She'd been foolish enough to leave off her collar, too. Only she hadn't the will you have, the will to flash and fight. It's what saved you."

Zena's mind went, *Will/won't. Will/won't.*

"What?" the man asked. Evidently she had said it aloud.

"Will," Zena whispered. "Only I didn't save me. You did."

"No, Zena, we could never have gotten to you in time if you hadn't screamed. Without the collar, Wild Wood Central can't track you. He counted on that."

"Track me?" Zena, unthinking, put a hand to her neck, found a bandage there.

"We try to keep a careful accounting of everything that goes on in the park," the man said. He looked, Zena thought, pretty coolish in his camouflage. Interesting looking, too, his face all planes and angles, with a wild, brushy orange mustache. Almost like one of those old pirates.

"Why?" she asked.

"Now that the city is safe everywhere else, people go Wilding just to feel that little shiver of fear. Just to get in touch with their primal selves."

"'Mime the prime,'" Zena said, remembering one of the old commercials.

"Exactly." He smiled. It was a very coolish smile. "And it's our job to make that fear safe. Control the chaos. Keep prime time clean."

"Then that guy . . ." Zena began, shuddering as she recalled the black mask, the hands around her neck.

"He'd actually killed three other girls, the Maharish girl being his latest. All girls without collars who didn't have the human fight-back knowhow. He'd gotten in unchanged through one of the old tunnels that we should have had blocked. 'Those wild girls,' he called his victims. Thanks to you, we caught him."

"Are you a cop?" Zena wrinkled her nose a bit.

"Nope. I'm a Max," he said, giving her a long, slow wink.

"A Max?"

"We control the Wild Things!" When she looked blank, he said, "It's an old story." He handed her a card. "In case you want to know more."

Zena looked at the card. It was embellished with holograms, front and back, of extinct animals. His name, Carl Barkham, was emblazoned in red across the elephant.

Just then her mother came in. Barkham greeted her with a mock salute and left. He walked down the hall with a deliberate, rangy stride that made him look, Zena thought, a lot like a powerful animal. A lion. Or a tiger.

"Princess!" her mother cried. "I came as soon as I heard."

"I'm fine, Mom," Zena said, not even wincing at the old nickname.

Behind her were Marnie, Lazlo, and Nick. They stood silently by the bed. At last Nick whispered, "You OK?" Somehow he seemed small, young, boneless. He was glancing nervously at Zena, at her mother, then back again. It was very uncoolish.

"I'm fine," Zena said. "Just a little achey." If Barkham was a tiger, then Nick was just a cub. "But I realize now that going collarless was really dumb. I was plain lucky."

"Coolish," Nick said.

But it wasn't. The Max was coolish. Nick was just . . . just . . . foolish.

"I'm ready to go home, Mom," Zena said. "I've got a lot of homework."

"Homework?" The word fell out of Nick's slack mouth.

She smiled pityingly at him, put her feet over the side of the bed, and stood. "I've got a lot of studying to do if I want to become a Max."

"What's a Max?" all four of them asked at once.

"Someone who tames the Wild Things," she said. "It's an old story. Come on, Mom. I'm starving. Got anything still hot for dinner?" ∿

Author's Note

I was born and brought up in New York City and lived most of the first thirteen years of my life in an apartment house on the corner of Central Park West and Ninety-Seventh Street, right next to the First Church of Christian Science. That is the exact setting of Wild Wood Central. *My brother and best friend, Diane, and I used to play in the park where Zena and her pals go, though we played baseball, cowboys and Indians, and Knights of the Round Table, not Wilding.*

The reference to Max and the Wild Things being "an old story" is, of course, a nod to Maurice Sendak's picture book Where the Wild Things Are. *It is a story in which a child's wildness is tamed by his imagination, which is a healthy outlet for that kind of thing. However, the actual term Wilding was one that arose in the late 1980s, when gangs of teenagers and young adults ran savagely though Central Park, mugging, raping, and beating up people whose only sin was to be in the wrong place at the wrong time. I'd like to think that we can tame our wildness or at least channel it into more acceptable behaviors, and my story is about that possibility.*

ALLEN GRESHNER

MEL GLENN

"Hello."
　　Pause, skin tight, small planet orbiting the sun,
　　flash of her smile, freckle, worried she'll say
　　yes, worried she'll say no,
"Tracy, This is Allen."
　　Lovely name, I'll marry her, stomach tight, voice
　　cracking, do it already, don't hang up, get to the
　　point, pause,
"Would you like to go to the prom with me?"
　　Guillotine blade, pause, hates me, fill the space,
　　no better than no sound, small hope, sinking,
"Can't make it?"
　　Why, what's wrong, what's wrong with me, big feet,
　　who else can I ask, hate proms, sweaty tux, sounded
　　too young, stomach churning,
"I understand."
　　No, I don't, don't choke, be cool, sound mature,
　　black hole in the universe, nothing ever goes right
　　for me, alone, relieved,
"Good night."

Search and Rescue

Tim Cahill

Park Country Search and Rescue called me out just before midnight on a cold November evening. The hunter had been missing for forty hours. He'd been working Tom Miner Basin, in the mountains adjacent to Yellowstone Park, tracking elk, his partner said. It was now about two in the morning, and the temperature had plunged to almost 30 degrees below zero. A local outfitter had volunteered his cabin near the trailhead, and that's where we were, poring over topographical maps, matching the terrain with what we knew of the hunter.

He was from out of state and didn't know the Montana mountains, his partner said, but he'd done some snow camping on the West Coast—Mount Rainier, I think. The guy went up alone, just to test himself in the snow. He was a highly trained security guard at the sort of facility terrorists target, and he kept himself in shape. We knew that while he didn't have a tent or sleeping bag, he did have matches, good boots, warm gloves and a good hat, and had dressed in woolen layers.

His partner said he was the type of guy who pushed himself, who didn't give up. They'd come across some elk tracks in the snow two days ago, and our lost hunter thought he could run the animals down. His partner waited at the trailhead until long after dark. Then he drove down into town and notified the sheriff.

Our team called the man's wife. You hate to do that—wake them up at two in the morning to tell them a loved one is missing in bitterly cold weather. And yet you have to know as much as you can. You have to figure out what your man is likely to do. The hunter had told his wife there was no way he could get lost. "All you have to do," he had said, "is walk downhill to the river." Near Tom Miner Basin, there are lots of ways to go downhill into places that lead straight back up into the spine of the Gallatin Mountains.

So that's what we had to work with: Tough guy, in shape, no quitter, some experience in the snow. I had a good feeling about this one. Mostly, after forty hours in 30 degrees-below-zero weather, they don't make it.

Our team was working from what we call the PLS—place last seen. Usually, after a day and a half, we'll find lost folks within a radius of about three miles of the PLS. For this hunter, we'd stretch the radius out to five miles. We figured our man must have followed the elk until it got dark on him that first night. The animals were moving south and west. We eliminated unlikely elk habitat, and established two or three areas where the man might have stood as the darkness fell on him. If he was disoriented and tried moving downhill, he could have ended up in only a few places.

In the morning, we'd send snowmobilers out into the areas where we least expected to find our man. It's tough searching for someone on a snow machine, and we don't put much faith in them. A horseback team would ride the search area diagonally, looking to cut tracks. A fixed-wing aircraft would overfly the basin.

Everything we knew about the hunter's personality, and the behavior of the elk he was tracking, suggested that the topography of the land

would funnel him into an area several miles away, at the top of an old logging road, somewhere near eight thousand feet. That's where we'd set up our base camp. We called in the county snowplow to clear the road. I saw it lumbering by the outfitter's cabin, its yellow revolving light casting eerie stroboscopic[1] shadows on the snow. At dawn, we'd dispatch half a dozen teams of two each to search the area on foot. That's what I'd volunteered to do. I'm what they call a ground pounder.

At four that morning, I laid out my sleeping bag in a back room and tried to get a few hours of sleep.

▲   ▲   ▲

We live in a world in which nothing that happens is our own fault. Slapstick has outlived its day. A slip on a banana peel isn't funny anymore—it's a lawsuit. Take Chiquita Banana to court on that one. We have all become victims.

Which, I think, is why some of us venture into the wilderness. We do so because it's not safe, and there's no one to blame but ourselves. You can get hurt out there, which is precisely the point. Wilderness is a way of taking back control of our lives.

When I first moved to the mountains almost twenty years ago, I lived on a remote ranch along a body of water called Poison Creek. The previous owner, an old-time cattle rancher named Don Hindman, had kept a thirty-acre portion of the land where he built a house in the shadow of the Crazy Mountains. Don was my mentor, and I used to walk the mile or so to his house every few days to visit and listen to stories.

One warm October day, I walked up to Don's house in my shirtsleeves. He asked if I'd considered the weather. Mountain weather, he pointed out, is frenetically variable. Temperatures can change 50, 70, even 100 degrees in twenty-four hours.

So, my mentor told me, even if you're only walking a mile on a sunny fall day, it's worth your life to be prepared. "Wear a coat," Don advised, adding, in his kindly avuncular[2] way, "you imbecile." During my first years in the mountains, I did a lot of these imbecilic things. Obviously, I survived. That's why it's called dumb luck. I figure I owe something to the wilderness, and that something is called Search and Rescue.

1 **stroboscopic:** flashing.
2 **avuncular:** like an uncle.

▲ ▲ ▲

Tom Miner Basin, in south-central Montana, is just north of the 45th parallel, about halfway between the equator and the North Pole. The mountains that rise on all sides reach altitudes of eleven and twelve thousand feet. To the west are the Gallatin Mountains; to the east, the Absarokas; to the north, the Crazy Mountains and the Bridgers.

For the most part, these mountain ranges are either managed wild lands or designated wilderness areas. They stretch into the adjoining states of Wyoming and Idaho and comprise the largest essentially intact ecosystem[3] in the "temperate zone"of the Northern Hemisphere. Called the Greater Yellowstone ecosystem, the rugged glaciated[4] mountains, high benches, and rolling prairies encompass millions of acres of state forest, national forest, and national parks, including Yellowstone National Park, Grand Teton National Park, and the 900,000-acre Absaroka-Beartooth Wilderness.

If I walked up into the mountains I can see from the front door of my house in town, I could hike seventy very rough miles until I even crossed a road. It ain't Disneyland out here, and the wilderness is not tolerant of mistakes.

There was, for instance, a young man who took a fatal fall near the summit of a mountain in the Beartooth Wilderness. In his tent, we found a bag of psychedelic mushrooms[5] and a notebook full of swirling spiral designs, which contained this terrifying note: "I think I can fly."

One year, two eighteen-year-old college coeds set out on a day trip to a lake at nine thousand feet. They were novice backpackers, and it was only five miles from the trailhead to the lake. They assumed they could walk ten miles in five hours, easy, but they hadn't calibrated three thousand feet of elevation into their plan. When it got dark, they stayed where they were, as they had been taught to do in a backpacking course. (Lost hunters, by contrast, usually strike out cross-country, and tracking them sometimes turns into a foot race.) We found the young women and got them down to the trailhead before dawn. Two sets of very happy parents were waiting there, and I felt about as good as I ever have in my life. The two girls were young enough to be my own daughters.

3 **ecosystem:** interrelated community of plants and animals.

4 **glaciated:** affected by glaciers—rivers of ice.

5 **psychedelic mushrooms:** mushrooms that cause delirium and hallucinations when eaten.

It doesn't always work out that well. A few years earlier, I was called out to search for two elk hunters in the Pine Creek Drainage. The men were friends, recent arrivals from Oregon, and not used to Rocky Mountain weather. They were hardworking fellows, barely scraping by on low-paying jobs, and both had families to feed. An elk—or two—would get them through the winter. They were meat hunters and honorable men.

The November day they set off dawned bright and clear. It was about 28 degrees above zero that morning. The men were dressed in cotton: denim jackets; denim pants. One of them had thought to wear a hat.

By sundown that evening, the temperature had dropped 50 degrees. A blinding snowstorm had closed down the entire county.

Why hadn't the men come out ahead of the snow? We tracked them for the better part of a day. The going was slow at first. Tom Murphy, our best man tracker, started from the trailhead, where the men had parked their vehicle. They had walked uphill, through wet snow covered over with the light airy snow that fell during the storm. It was necessary to crawl along the men's direction of travel, blowing powder—blue smoke, we call it—out of the tracks in the older hard-packed snow.

Early the first afternoon, the tracks said, the men had shot an elk. Apparently they tried to drag the 600- or 700-pound animal toward their vehicle. It would have been sweaty work, even in the cold. Their cotton clothes were likely soaked.

Sometime late that afternoon, as the temperature dropped, they must have realized they were in trouble. They left the elk and tried to walk out. But the blizzard was on them, and they appeared to be disoriented. Their tracks, easier to follow now in the deep newly fallen snow, veered off from the place where their vehicle was parked. They began moving downhill, but the heavily wooded slope steepened precipitously. The forest was dense with trees, thick with down timber.

It must have seemed hopeless in that storm, in the dark, with no lights. The snow was knee- and thigh-deep, and the men left tracks like post holes. Twice they stopped and tried to light a fire. Both times they failed. It was 25 degrees below zero that night.

We stood looking at the burned matches and the green living boughs the men had tried to ignite. The downed trees on either side would have provided plenty of tinder, but the men tried to burn green pine boughs instead. They were experienced woodsmen—former loggers—and knew

6 **hypothermia:** condition caused by subnormal body temperature.

how to build a fire. While they had been working with the elk, hypothermia[6] had ambushed them. We could see it in their tracks—in their lack of coordination and their confusion, in their stumbling pace, in the bad decisions they made, in the few cold ashes of their failed fires.

One set of tracks led over a fallen tree and stopped. The man had fallen backward, and was caught in a sitting position, with his arm entangled in the branches of a living tree. He died there, in that place, and his sweat-soaked clothes were frozen stiff on his body.

Another set of tracks approached the fatal tree, and there was an indentation in the snow where the second man had sat down. The two must have talked there, in the dark, with the snow falling all around them. They must have known they were dying.

We found the second man half a mile away. The tracks in the snow said that he sat down, smoked one last cigarette, then pitched over and died.

To this day, I'm haunted by those tracks. Several times over the past few years I've dreamed of those men and of that last conversation.

▲ ▲ ▲

I was trying to sleep in the outfitter's cabin when I saw the yellow light on the snowplow moving back down the gravel road leading to town. In another few hours, I'd be out pounding the ground, looking for the lost security guard. I needed to sleep, and just as I was dozing off, some bozo started hammering on the front door. I heard someone mutter and stir. There was the sound of a door opening.

A sheriff's deputy said, "Oh man, are we glad to see you."

And a man's voice—raspy, exhausted—replied, "You think you're glad?"

We kind of like it when the lost hunters find us.

I stoked up the woodstove, and our man sat in front of it for fifteen minutes before we could get the frozen boots off his feet. There were no signs of frostbite. The guy would keep all his fingers and his toes. He'd built a few fires, he said, but they hadn't kept him

very warm. He'd been working on a new plan—two fires: one at his back; one at his front—when he saw the strange yellow light flashing on the snow far below. He'd run stumbling, down the steep snow-slope, but the plow was gone long before he got there. He'd followed its track down the logging road and knocked on the door of the first cabin he saw. Which was where we were.

The man called his wife. I had the feeling, from listening to his end of the conversation, that she was crying. His partner walked around shaking our hands. He kept saying, "I can't believe you sent the plow right to him." We were sort of proud of that ourselves.

Later, just at dawn, I took a short walk in the snow and stood overlooking the Yellowstone Valley. Our lost hunter had been pretty good out there, and I tried to see the sunrise through his eyes. Far below, I could mark the course of the river by the fog rising off fast-moving water. The air glittered with tiny floating crystals of ice, called diamond dust, and when I looked into the sun, it was haloed in rainbows. The last few days had been a matter of life or death for our guy—for all of us—and that, I thought, is both the secret and the terrible beauty of wilderness. It was going to be an absolutely splendid day, and we had no one to blame for that but ourselves. ∾

Winterstorm, Yosemite National Park 1944 Ansel Adams.

THE FINE MADNESS
OF IDITAROD

GARY PAULSEN

I do not hold the record for the person coming to disaster soonest in the Iditarod.[1] There have been some mushers who have never left the chutes. Their dogs dove into the spectators or turned back on the team and tried to go out of the chutes backwards. But I rank close.

We made almost two blocks. The distance before the first turn. Wilson (the lead dog) ran true down the track left by the previous thirty-one teams. Until the turn. At the end of two blocks there was a hard turn to the right to head down a side street, then out of town on back trails and alleys and into the trees along the highways away from Anchorage.

I remember watching the turn coming at alarming speed. All the dogs were running wide open and I thought that the only way to make it was to lean well to the right, my weight far out to the side to keep the sled from tumbling and rolling. I prepared, leaned out and into the turn and would have been fine except that Wilson did not take the turn. He kept going straight, blew on through the crowd and headed off into Anchorage on his own tour of discovery.

We went through people's yards, ripped down fences, knocked over garbage cans. At one point I found myself going through a carport and across a backyard with fifteen dogs and a fully loaded Iditarod sled. A woman standing over the kitchen sink looked out with wide eyes as we passed through her yard and I snapped a wave at her before clawing the

1 **Iditarod:** an annual sled dog race from Anchorage to Nome, Alaska.

A sled dog race begins in Anchorage, Alaska.

handlebar again to hang on while we tore down her picket fence when Wilson tried to thread through a hole not much bigger than a housecat. And there is a cocker spaniel who will never come into his backyard again. He heard us coming and turned to bark just as the entire team ran over him; I flipped one of the runners up to just miss his back and we were gone, leaving him standing facing the wrong way barking at whatever it was that had hit him.

I heard later that at the banquet some people had been speaking of me and I was unofficially voted the least likely to get out of Anchorage. Bets were made on how soon I would crash and burn. Two blocks, three. Some said one. It was very nearly true.

Back on the streets I started hooking signs with the snowhook. They were flimsy and bent when the hook hit them and I despaired of ever stopping, but at last my luck turned and the hook caught on a stop sign just right and hung and held the team while I put Cookie back in the lead and moved Wilson—still grinning wildly and snorting steam and ready to rip—back into the team.

I now had control but was completely lost and found myself in the dubious position of having to stop along the street and ask gawking bystanders if they knew the way to the Iditarod trail.

"Well, sure I do. You take this street down four blocks, then cross by the small metal culvert and catch the walking path through the park there until you see the gas station with the old Ford parked out front where you hang a kind of oblique right . . . ."

It is a miracle that I ever got out of town. Finally I reasoned that I had fallen somehow north of the trail and I headed in a southerly direction and when we had gone a mile or so Cookie put her nose down and suddenly hung a left into some trees, around a sharp turn and I saw sled runner marks and we were back on the trail. (As we moved into this small stand of birch and spruce I saw shattered remnants of a sled in the trees and found later that a man had cracked the whip on the turn and hit the trees and broken his leg and had to scratch.[2] He was not the first one to scratch; there had already been two others who gave it up before getting out of town.)

I was four-and-a-half hours getting to the first official checkpoint at Eagle River—a suburb of Anchorage—where I was met by the handlers and (my wife) Ruth. We had to unhook the dogs and put them in the

2 **scratch:** quit.

truck and drive on the freeway to where the race truly starts, at Knik, on the edge of the bush.

"How's it going?" Ruth asked as I loaded the dogs.

"After this it ought to be all downhill," I said. "Nothing can be as hard as getting out of town . . ."

▲　▲　▲

In the pre-race briefing, we had been told in general about some of the more difficult hardships of the race—the mountains, the interior, the cold.

At that time, someone had momentarily mentioned Happy Canyon. We were told that it lay between Finger Lake and Rainy Pass—comparable to stating that New York City lies between Boston and Washington, D.C.—and that it might prove difficult because of deep snow. Or something. I had written it down but had forgotten what I'd written.

We were not told that it was a near-vertical drop down a cliff, nor that it came soon after Finger Lake, when the dogs were still rested and fresh.

I was doing something in the sled—tightening a lashing—and I looked up to see the front end of the team suddenly drop off the edge of the world.

The morning had dawned clear, but a wind had come up, blowing new snow in swirling clouds. I could not at first see where the dogs had gone because of this, but as I rapidly approached the drop point, watching each set of dogs drop out of sight, the wind eddied and momentarily cleared, and I got my first true look at Happy Canyon.

I am not religious but I think I would have prayed had there been more time. Spread out below me, as far as I could see, was an enormous canyon. The far side seemed miles away and the river down below a tiny line in the middle.

"S—" I had time for the one word . . . and then the sled, pulled by the now falling team, came to the drop-off.

I honestly do not know how I made it. Later, I was speaking to an Englishman who had run the race, and in typical British understatement, he said, "It's rather like falling, isn't it?"

Plummeting would be more the word. There was something approximating a ledge-trail that went down to an impossibly abrupt switchback, but the trail didn't matter.

Cookie, realizing that to survive she would have to stay ahead of the suddenly falling team, sled, and musher, said to heck with the trail and

jumped off the edge, aimed straight down. The team, used to following her blindly, jumped off after her.

I grabbed the handlebar of the sled with both hands and hung on, dragging on my stomach as we careened, flopped, rolled, and tumbled some five hundred feet down to the frozen river below.

I would like to say that because I kept my wits about me and was cool in the face of a crisis, I used my body as a living sled drag, which kept the sled from running over the dogs, and through a series of delicately performed maneuvers, we came smoothly to a stop on the river ice below.

I would like to say that, but it would be a lie. While in reality that is exactly what happened, it was all accidental. As soon as we started down, I closed my eyes, I may have screamed, as two mushers who were on the ice repairing broken sleds said, but I can't remember doing so. When I opened them, I was lying on the river ice, the dogs were lined up in front of me perfectly, and the sled—wonder of wonders—was upright and all the gear intact.

Off to the side, the two mushers stood clapping softly. One of them smiled and nodded. "Far out—I'm going to do it that way next year."

I stood, shook the snow from my clothing, and shrugged. "I didn't know any other way to play it."

"Right."

"Dumb luck . . ."

At that he nodded and was going to say more except that we heard a bellow and turned to see what appeared to be a lumber yard exploding as the next team came over the edge. Gear, bits of sled, dogs, man, odds and ends of clothing all came down in a roiling mass of barks and screamed curses.

I set my hook and helped the other two men catch the dogs and relocate the gear. The musher, a short-set man who had run the race several times, nodded and smiled at me. "Don't you just *love* this race?"

And I was taken aback to realize that he truly meant it—he really loved the race. Here was a man who had run the race several times, had never won, never even been in the money (they pay down twenty places), and he truly loved the race.

I mumbled something to him and lined my team out and left. Had I thought on it, considered my own feelings, I would have recognized that I was coming to be the same way. The race was already becoming an entity to me—becoming more than a sum of its parts—was becoming The Iditarod. ∾

RESPONDING TO CLUSTER ONE

WHY DO PEOPLE TAKE RISKS?

Thinking Skill HYPOTHESIZING

1. Does a rescuer need to be a risk taker? Be prepared to explain your answer. You might construct a chart such as the one below to record your thinking.

Rescuer	Qualities
The Max in "Wilding"	
Tim Cahill in "Search and Rescue"	
Rescuers you may have seen or read about	

2. What four items would you take with you into the winter wilderness, and why?

3. **Hypothesize** (make a logical explanation) about what Paulsen could do to improve his chances the next time he runs the Iditarod. Be prepared to support your answer with details from the text.

4. Both Zena in "Wilding" and Allen Greshner in the poem go through painful experiences. In your opinion, are painful experiences a necessary part of growing up? Explain your response by using details from the selections or from your own experiences.

Writing Activity: Hypothesizing About Why People Take Risks

Write a hypothesis that explains why some people take risks. Support your hypothesis with observations from the selections or from your own experiences.

A Strong Hypothesis

• begins with an intelligent guess or theory

• is based on observations and experiences

• can be tested by observing and recording information

CLUSTER TWO

AFTER SURVIVING?

Thinking Skill   GENERALIZING

CONTENTS OF THE DEAD MAN'S POCKETS

JACK FINNEY

At the little living-room desk Tom Benecke rolled two sheets of flimsy and a heavier top sheet, carbon paper[1] sandwiched between them, into his portable. *Inter-office Memo,*[2] the top sheet was headed, and he typed tomorrow's date just below this; then he glanced at a creased yellow sheet, covered with his own handwriting, beside the typewriter. "Hot in here," he muttered to himself. Then, from the short hallway at his back, he heard the muffled clang of wire coat hangers in the bedroom closet, and at this reminder of what his wife was doing he thought: Hot, no—guilty conscience.

He got up, shoving his hands into the back pockets of his gray wash slacks, stepped to the living-room window beside the desk and stood breathing on the glass, watching the expanding circlet of mist, staring down through the autumn night at Lexington Avenue, eleven stories below. He was a tall, lean, dark-haired young man in a pullover sweater, who looked as though he had played not football, probably, but basketball in college. Now he placed the heels of his hands against the top edge of the lower window frame and shoved upwards. But as usual the window didn't budge, and he had to lower his hands and then shoot them hard upwards to jolt the window open a few inches. He dusted his hands, muttering.

1 **carbon paper:** thin ink-covered paper used to make an identical copy of typewritten text.
2 *Inter-office Memo:* in business, a short note or reminder sent from one department to another.

But still he didn't begin his work. He crossed the room to the hallway entrance and, leaning against the doorjamb, hands shoved into his back pockets again, he called, "Clare?" When his wife answered, he said, "Sure you don't mind going alone?"

"No." Her voice was muffled, and he knew her head and shoulders were in the bedroom closet. Then the tap of her high heels sounded on the wood floor and she appeared at the end of the little hallway, wearing a slip, both hands raised to one ear, clipping on an earring. She smiled at him—a slender, very pretty girl with light brown, almost blond, hair—her prettiness emphasized by the pleasant nature that showed in her face. "It's just that I hate you to miss this movie; you wanted to see it, too."

"Yeah, I know." He ran his fingers through his hair. "Got to get this done, though."

She nodded, accepting this. Then, glancing at the desk across the living room, she said, "You work too much, though, Tom—and too hard."

He smiled. "You won't mind, though, will you, when the money comes rolling in and I'm known as the Boy Wizard of Wholesale Groceries?"

"I guess not." She smiled and turned back toward the bedroom.

At his desk again, Tom lighted a cigarette; then a few moments later, as Clare appeared dressed and ready to leave, he set it on the rim of the ashtray. "Just after seven," she said. "I can make the beginning of the first feature."[3]

He walked to the front-door closet to help her on with her coat. He kissed her then and, for an instant, holding her close, smelling the perfume she had used, he was tempted to go with her; it was not actually true that he had to work tonight, though he very much wanted to. This was his own project, unannounced as yet in his office, and it could be postponed. But then they won't see it till Monday, he thought once again, and if I give it to the boss tomorrow he might read it over the weekend. . . . "Have a good time," he said aloud. He gave his wife a little swat and opened the door for her, feeling the air from the building hallway, smelling faintly of floor wax, stream gently past his face.

He watched her walk down the hall, flicked a hand in response as she waved, and then he started to close the door, but it resisted for a

---

3 **first feature:** first movie of a "double feature" (two full-length movies viewed for one admission price).

moment. As the door opening narrowed, the current of warm air from the hallway, channeled through this smaller opening now, suddenly rushed past him with accelerated force. Behind him he heard the slap of the window curtains against the wall and the sound of paper fluttering from his desk, and he had to push to close the door.

Turning, he saw a sheet of white paper drifting to the floor in a series of arcs, and another sheet, yellow, moving towards the window, caught in the dying current flowing through the narrow opening. As he watched, the paper struck the bottom edge of the window and hung there for an instant, plastered against the glass and wood. Then as the moving air stilled completely, the curtains swinging back from the wall to hang free again, he saw the yellow sheet drop to the window ledge and slide over out of sight.

▲   ▲   ▲

He ran across the room, grasped the bottom of the window and tugged, staring through the glass. He saw the yellow sheet, dimly now in the darkness outside, lying on the ornamental ledge a yard below the window. Even as he watched, it was moving, scraping slowly along the ledge, pushed by the breeze that pressed steadily against the building wall. He heaved on the window with all his strength, and it shot open with a bang, the window weight rattling in the casing. But the paper was past his reach and, leaning out into the night, he watched it scud steadily along the ledge to the south, half plastered against the building wall. Above the muffled sound of the street traffic far below, he could hear the dry scrape of its movement, like a leaf on the pavement.

The living room of the next apartment to the south projected a yard or more farther out towards the street than this one; because of this the Beneckes paid seven and a half dollars less rent than their neighbors. And now the yellow sheet, sliding along the stone ledge, nearly invisible in the night, was stopped by the projecting blank wall of the next apartment. It lay motionless then, in the corner formed by the two walls a good five yards away, pressed firmly against the ornate corner ornament of the ledge by the breeze that moved past Tom Benecke's face.

He knelt at the window and stared at the yellow paper for a full minute or more, waiting for it to move, to slide off the ledge and fall, hoping he could follow its course to the street, and then hurry down in the elevator and retrieve it. But it didn't move, and then he saw that the paper was caught firmly between a projection of the convoluted corner ornament and the ledge. He thought about the poker from the fireplace, then the broom, then the mop—discarding each thought as it occurred to him. There was nothing in the apartment long enough to reach that paper.

It was hard for him to understand that he actually had to abandon it—it was ridiculous—and he began to curse. Of all the papers on his desk, why did it have to be this one in particular! On four long Saturday afternoons he had stood in supermarkets, counting the people who passed certain displays, and the results were scribbled on that yellow sheet. From stacks of trade publications, gone over page by page in snatched half hours at work and during evenings at home, he had copied facts, quotations, and figures onto that sheet. And he had carried it with him to the Public Library on Fifth Avenue, where he'd spent a dozen lunch hours and early evenings adding more. All were needed to support and lend authority to his idea for a new grocery-store display method; without them his idea was a mere opinion. And there they all lay, in his own improvised shorthand—countless hours of work—out there on the ledge.

For many seconds he believed he was going to abandon the yellow sheet, that there was nothing else to do. The work could be duplicated. But it would take two months, and the time to present this idea was now, for use in the spring displays. He struck his fist on the window ledge. Then he shrugged. Even though his plan was adopted, he told himself, it wouldn't bring him a raise in pay—not immediately, anyway, or as a direct result. It won't bring me a promotion either, he argued—not of itself.

But just the same, and he couldn't escape the thought, this and other independent projects, some already done and others planned for the future, would gradually mark him out from the score of other young men in his company. They were the ways to change from a name on the payroll to a name in the minds of the company officials. They were the beginning of the long, long climb to where he was determined to be—at the very top. And he knew he was going out there in the darkness, after the yellow sheet fifteen feet beyond his reach.

By a kind of instinct, he instantly began making his intention acceptable to himself by laughing at it. The mental picture of himself sidling along the ledge outside was absurd—it was actually comical—and he smiled. He imagined himself describing it; it would make a good story at the office and, it occurred to him, would add a special interest and importance to his memorandum, which would do it no harm at all.

To simply go out and get his paper was an easy task—he could be back here with it in less than two minutes—and he knew he wasn't deceiving himself. The ledge, he saw, measuring it with his eye, was about as wide as the length of his shoe, and perfectly flat. And every fifth row of brick in the face of the building, he remembered—leaning out, he verified this—was indented half an inch, enough for the tips of his fingers, enough to maintain balance easily. It occurred to him that if this ledge and wall were only a yard above ground—as he knelt at the window staring out, this thought was the final confirmation of his intention—he could move along the ledge indefinitely.

On a sudden impulse, he got to his feet, walked to the front closet and took out an old tweed jacket; it would be cold outside. He put it on and buttoned it as he crossed the room rapidly towards the open window. In the back of his mind he knew he'd better hurry and get this over with before he thought too much, and at the window he didn't allow himself to hesitate.

He swung a leg over the sill, then felt for and found the ledge a yard below the window with his foot. Gripping the bottom of the window frame very tightly and carefully, he slowly ducked his head under it, feeling on his face the sudden change from the warm air of the room to the chill outside. With infinite care he brought out his other leg, his mind concentrating on what he was doing. Then he slowly stood erect. Most of the putty, dried out and brittle, had dropped off the bottom edging of the window frame, he found, and the flat wooden edging provided a good gripping surface, a half inch or more deep, for the tips of his fingers.

Now, balanced easily and firmly, he stood on the ledge outside in the slight, chill breeze, eleven stories above the street, staring into his own lighted apartment, odd and different-seeming now.

First his right hand, then his left, he carefully shifted his finger-tip grip from the puttyless window edging to an indented row of bricks directly to his right. It was hard to take the first shuffling sideways step then—to make himself move—and the fear stirred in his stomach, but he did it, again by not allowing himself time to think. And now—with his chest, stomach, and the left side of his face pressed against the rough cold brick—his lighted apartment was suddenly gone, and it was much darker out here than he had thought.

Without pause he continued—right foot, left foot, right foot, left—his shoe soles shuffling and scraping along the rough stone, never lifting from it, fingers sliding along the exposed edging of brick. He moved on the balls of his feet, heels lifted slightly; the ledge was not quite as wide as he'd expected. But leaning slightly inward towards the face of the building and pressed against it, he could feel his balance firm and secure, and moving along the ledge was quite as easy as he had thought it would be. He could hear the buttons of his jacket scraping steadily along the rough bricks and feel them catch momentarily, tugging a little, at each mortared crack. He simply did not permit himself to look down, though the compulsion to do so never left him; nor did he allow himself actually to think. Mechanically—right foot, left foot, over and again—he shuffled along crabwise, watching the projecting wall ahead loom steadily closer. . . .

Then he reached it and, at the corner—he'd decided how he was going to pick up the paper—he lifted his right foot and placed it carefully on the ledge that ran along the projecting wall at a right angle to the ledge on which his other foot rested. And now, facing the building, he stood in the corner formed by the two walls, one foot on the ledging of each, a hand on the shoulder-high indentation of each wall. His forehead was pressed directly into the corner against the cold bricks, and now he carefully lowered first one hand, then the other, perhaps a foot farther down, to the next indentation in the rows of bricks.

▲ ▲ ▲

Very slowly, sliding his forehead down the trough of the brick corner and bending his knees, he lowered his body towards the paper lying between his outstretched feet. Again he lowered his fingerholds another foot and bent his knees still more, thigh muscles taut, his forehead sliding and bumping down the brick V. Half squatting now, he dropped his left hand to the next indentation and then slowly reached with his right hand towards the paper between his feet.

He couldn't quite touch it, and his knees now were pressed against the wall; he could bend them no farther. But by ducking his head another inch lower, the top of his head now pressed against the bricks, he lowered his right shoulder and his fingers had the paper by a corner, pulling it loose. At the same instant he saw, between his legs and far below, Lexington Avenue stretched out for miles ahead.

He saw, in that instant, the Loew's theatre sign, blocks ahead past Fiftieth Street; the miles of traffic signals, all green now; the lights of cars and street lamps; countless neon signs; and the moving black dots of

CORNICE
1949 George Tooker

people. And a violent, instantaneous explosion of absolute terror roared through him. For a motionless instant he saw himself externally—bent practically double, balanced on this narrow ledge, nearly half his body projecting out above the street far below—and he began to tremble violently, panic flaring through his mind and muscles, and he felt the blood rush from the surface of his skin.

In the fractional moment before horror paralyzed him, as he stared between his legs at that terrible length of street far beneath him, a fragment of his mind raised his body in a spasmodic jerk to an upright position again, but so violently that his head scraped hard against the wall, bouncing off it, and his body swayed outwards to the knife edge of balance, and he very nearly plunged backwards and fell. Then he was leaning far into the corner again, squeezing and pushing into it, not only his face but his chest and stomach, his back arching; and his finger tips clung with all the pressure of his pulling arms to the shoulder-high half-inch indentation in the bricks.

He was more than trembling now; his whole body was racked with a violent shuddering beyond control, his eyes squeezed so tightly shut it was painful, though he was past awareness of that. His teeth were exposed in a frozen grimace, the strength draining like water from his knees and calves. It was extremely likely, he knew, that he would faint, slump down along the wall, his face scraping, and then drop backwards, a limp weight, out into nothing. And to save his life he concentrated on holding on to consciousness, drawing deliberate deep breaths of cold air into his lungs, fighting to keep his senses aware.

Then he knew that he would not faint, but he could not stop shaking nor open his eyes. He stood where he was, breathing deeply, trying to hold back the terror of the glimpse he had had of what lay below him; and he knew he had made a mistake in not making himself stare down at the street, getting used to it and accepting it, when he had first stepped out onto the ledge.

It was impossible to walk back. He simply could not do it. He couldn't bring himself to make the slightest movement. The strength was gone from his legs; his shivering hands—numb, cold, and desperately rigid— had lost all deftness; his easy ability to move and balance was gone. Within a step or two, if he tried to move, he knew that he would stumble clumsily and fall.

Seconds passed, with the chill faint wind pressing the side of his face, and he could hear the toned-down volume of the street traffic far beneath him. Again and again it slowed and then stopped, almost to silence; then presently, even this high, he would hear the click of the traffic signals and the subdued roar of the cars starting up again. During a lull in the street sounds, he called out. Then he was shouting *"Help!"* so loudly it rasped his throat. But he felt the steady pressure of the wind, moving between his face and the blank wall, snatch up his cries as he uttered them, and he knew they must sound directionless and distant. And he remembered how habitually, here in New York, he himself heard and ignored shouts in the night. If anyone heard him, there was no sign of it, and presently Tom Benecke knew he had to try moving; there was nothing else he could do.

Eyes squeezed shut, he watched scenes in his mind like scraps of motion-picture film—he could not stop them. He saw himself stumbling suddenly sideways as he crept along the ledge and saw his upper body arc outwards, arms flailing. He saw a dangling shoestring caught between the ledge and the sole of his other shoe, saw a foot start to move, to be stopped with a jerk, and felt his balance leaving him. He saw himself falling with a terrible speed as his body revolved in the air, knees clutched tight to his chest, eyes squeezed shut, moaning softly.

Out of utter necessity, knowing that any of these thoughts might be reality in the very next seconds, he was slowly able to shut his mind against every thought but what he now began to do. With fear-soaked slowness, he slid his left foot an inch or two towards his own impossibly distant window. Then he slid the fingers of his shivering left hand a corresponding distance. For a moment he could not bring himself to lift his right foot from one ledge to the other; then he did it, and became aware of the harsh exhalation of air from his throat and realized that he was panting. As his right hand, then, began to slide along the brick edging, he was astonished to feel the yellow paper pressed to the bricks underneath his stiff fingers, and he uttered a terrible, abrupt bark that might have been a laugh or a moan. He opened his mouth and took the paper in his teeth, pulling it out from under his fingers.

By a kind of trick—by concentrating his entire mind on first his left foot, then his left hand, then the other foot, then the other hand—he was able to move, almost imperceptibly, trembling steadily, very nearly without thought. But he could feel the terrible strength of the pent-up horror on just the other side of the flimsy barrier he had erected in his mind; and he knew that if it broke through he would lose this thin, artificial control of his body.

During one slow step he tried keeping his eyes closed; it made him feel safer, shutting him off a little from the fearful reality of where he was. Then a sudden rush of giddiness swept over him, and he had to open his eyes wide, staring sideways at the cold rough brick and angled lines of mortar, his cheek tight against the building. He kept his eyes open then, knowing that if he once let them flick outwards, to stare for an instant at the lighted windows across the street, he would be past help.

He didn't know how many dozens of tiny sidling steps he had taken, his chest, belly, and face pressed to the wall; but he knew the slender hold he was keeping on his mind and body was going to break. He had a sudden mental picture of his apartment on just the other side of this wall—warm, cheerful, incredibly spacious. And he saw himself striding through it, lying down on the floor on his back, arms spread wide, revelling in its unbelievable security. The impossible remoteness of this utter safety, the contrast between it and where he now stood, was more than he could bear. And the barrier broke then, and the fear of the awful height he stood on coursed through his nerves and muscles.

A fraction of his mind knew he was going to fall, and he began taking rapid blind steps with no feeling of what he was doing, sidling with a clumsy, desperate swiftness, fingers scrabbling along the brick, almost hopelessly resigned to the sudden backward pull and swift motion outward and down. Then his moving hand slid onto not brick but sheer emptiness, an impossible gap in the face of the wall, and he stumbled.

His right foot smashed into his left ankle bone; he staggered sideways, began falling, and the claw of his hand cracked against glass and wood, slid down it, and his finger tips were pressed hard on the puttyless edging of his window. His right hand smacked gropingly beside it as he fell to his knees; and, under the full weight and direct downward pull of his sagging body, the open window dropped shudderingly in its frame till it closed and his wrists struck the sill and were jarred off.

For a single moment he knelt, knee bones against stone on the very edge of the ledge, body swaying and touching nowhere else, fighting for balance. Then he lost it, his shoulders plunging backwards, and he flung his arms forward, his hands smashing against the window casing on either side and—his body moving backwards—his fingers clutched the narrow wood stripping of the upper pane.

For an instant he hung suspended between balance and falling, his finger tips pressed onto the quarter-inch wood strips. Then, with utmost delicacy with a focused concentration of all his senses, he increased even further the strain on his finger tips hooked to these slim edgings of wood. Elbows slowly bending, he began to draw the full weight of his upper body forward, knowing that the instant his fingers slipped off these quarter-inch strips he'd plunge backwards and be falling. Elbows imperceptibly bending, body shaking with the strain, the sweat starting from his forehead in great sudden drops, he pulled, his entire being and thought concentrated in his finger tips. Then, suddenly, the strain slackened and ended, his chest touching the window sill, and he was kneeling on the ledge, his forehead pressed to the glass of the closed window.

Dropping his palms to the sill, he stared into his living room—at the red-brown davenport[4] across the room, and a magazine he had left there; at the pictures on the walls and the gray rug; the entrance to the hallway; and at his papers, typewriter, and desk, not two feet from his nose. A movement from his desk caught his eye, and he saw that it was a thin curl of blue smoke; his cigarette, the ash long, was still burning in the ashtray where he'd left it—this was past all belief—only a few minutes before.

His head moved, and in faint reflection from the glass before him, he saw the yellow paper clenched in his front teeth. Lifting a hand from the sill he took it from his mouth; the moistened corner parted from the paper, and he spat it out.

▲　▲　▲

For a moment, in the light from the living room, he stared wonderingly at the yellow sheet in his hand and then crushed it into the side pocket of his jacket.

He couldn't open the window. It had been pulled not completely closed, but its lower edge was below the level of the outside sill; there was no room to get his fingers underneath it. Between the upper sash and the lower was a gap not wide enough—reaching up, he tried—to get his fingers into; he couldn't push it open. The upper window panel, he knew from long experience, was impossible to move, frozen tight with dried paint.

Very carefully observing his balance, the finger tips of his left hand again hooked to the narrow stripping of the window casing, he drew his right hand, palm facing the glass, and then struck the glass with the heel of his hand.

His arm rebounded from the pane, his body tottering, and he knew he didn't dare strike a harder blow.

But in the security and relief of his new position, he simply smiled; with only a sheet of glass between him and the room just before him, it was not possible that there wasn't a way past it. Eyes narrowing, he thought for a few moments about what to do. Then his eyes widened, for nothing occurred to him. But still he felt calm: the trembling, he realized, had stopped. At the back of his mind there still lay the thought that once he was again in his home, he could give release to his feelings.

---

4 **davenport:** couch or sofa.

He actually *would* lie on the floor, rolling, clenching tufts of the rug in his hands. He would literally run across the room, free to move as he liked, jumping on the floor, testing and reveling in its absolute security, letting the relief flood through him, draining the fear from his mind and body. His yearning for this was astonishingly intense, and somehow he understood that he had better keep this feeling at bay.

He took a half dollar from his pocket and struck it against the pane, but without any hope that the glass would break and with very little disappointment when it did not. After a few moments of thought he drew his leg up on to the ledge and picked loose the knot of his shoe lace. He slipped off his shoe and, holding it across the instep, drew back his arm as far as he dared and struck the leather heel against the glass. The pane rattled, but he knew he'd been a long way from breaking it. His foot was cold and he slipped the shoe back on. He shouted again, experimentally, and then once more, but there was no answer.

The realization suddenly struck him that he might have to wait here till Clare came home, and for a moment the thought was funny. He could see Clare opening the front door, withdrawing her key from the lock, closing the door behind her, and then glancing up to see him crouch on the other side of the window. He could see her rush across the room, face astounded and frightened, and hear himself shouting instructions: "Never mind how I got here! Just open the wind—" She couldn't open it, he remembered, she'd never been able to; she'd always had to call him. She'd have to get the building superintendent or a neighbor, and he pictured himself smiling and answering their questions as he climbed in. "I just wanted to get a breath of fresh air, so—"

He couldn't possibly wait here till Clare came home. It was the second feature she'd wanted to see, and she'd left in time to see the first. She'd be another three hours or— He glanced at his watch; Clare had been gone eight minutes. It wasn't possible, but only eight minutes ago he had kissed his wife good-bye. She wasn't even in the theatre yet!

It would be four hours before she could possibly be home, and he tried to picture himself kneeling out here, finger tips hooked to these narrow strippings, while first one movie, preceded by a slow listing of credits, began, developed, reached its climax and then finally ended. There'd be a newsreel next, maybe, and then an animated cartoon, and then interminable scenes from coming pictures. And then, once more, the beginning of a full-length picture—while all the time he hung out here in the night.

He might possibly get to his feet, but he was afraid to try. Already his legs were cramped, his thigh muscles tired; his knees hurt, his feet felt numb, and his hands were stiff. He couldn't possibly stay out here for four hours or anywhere near it. Long before that his legs and arms would give out; he would be forced to try changing his position often—stiffly, clumsily, his coordination and strength gone—and he would fall. Quite realistically, he knew that he would fall; no one could stay out here on this ledge for four hours.

A dozen windows in the apartment building across the street were lighted. Looking over his shoulder, he could see the top of a man's head behind the newspaper he was reading; in another window he saw the blue-gray flicker of a television screen. No more than twenty-odd yards from his back were scores of people, and if just one of them would walk idly to his window and glance out. . . . For some moments he stared over his shoulder at the lighted rectangles, waiting. But no one appeared. The man reading his paper turned a page and then continued his reading. A figure passed another of the windows and was immediately gone.

In the inside pocket of his jacket he found a little sheaf of papers, and he pulled one out and looked at it in the light from the living room. It was an old letter, an advertisement of some sort; his name and address, in purple ink, were on a label pasted to the envelope. Gripping one end of the envelope in his teeth, he twisted it into a tight curl. From his shirt pocket he brought out a book of matches. He didn't dare let go the casing with both hands but, with the twist of paper in his teeth, he opened the match book with his free hand; then he bent one of the matches in two without tearing it from the folder, its red-tipped end now touching the striking surface. With his thumb, he rubbed the red tip across the striking area.

He did it again, then again, and still again, pressing harder each time, and the match suddenly flared, burning his thumb. But he kept it alight, cupping the match book in his hand and shielding it with his body. He held the flame to the paper in his mouth till it caught. Then he snuffed out the match flame with his thumb and forefinger careless of the burn, and replaced the book in his pocket. Taking the paper twist in his hand, he held it flame down, watching the flame crawl up the paper, till it flared bright. Then he held it behind him over the street, moving it from side to side, watching it over his shoulder, the flame flickering and guttering in the wind.

There were three letters in his pocket and he lighted each of them, holding each till the flame touched his hand and then dropping it to the street below. At one point, watching over his shoulder while the last of the letters burned, he saw the man across the street put down his paper and stand—even seeming, to Tom, to glance towards his window. But when he moved, it was only to walk across the room and disappear from sight.

There were a dozen coins in Tom Benecke's pocket and he dropped them, three or four at a time. But if they struck anyone or if anyone noticed their falling, no one connected them with their source, and no one glanced upwards.

His arms had begun to tremble from the steady strain of clinging to his narrow perch, and he did not know what to do now and was terribly frightened. Clinging to the window stripping with one hand, he again searched his pockets. But now—he had left his wallet on his dresser when he'd changed clothes—there was nothing left but the yellow sheet. It occurred to him irrelevantly that his death on the sidewalk below would be an eternal mystery; the window closed—why, how, and from where could he have fallen? No one would be able to identify his body for a time, either—the thought was somehow unbearable and increased his fear. All they'd find in his pockets would be the yellow sheet. *Contents of the dead man's pockets,* he thought, *one sheet of paper bearing penciled notations—incomprehensible.*

He understood fully that he might actually be going to die; his arms, maintaining his balance on the ledge, were trembling steadily now. And it occurred to him then with all the force of a revelation that, if he fell, all he was ever going to have out of life he would then, abruptly, have had. Nothing, then, could ever be changed; and nothing more—no least experience or pleasure—could ever be added to his life. He wished, then, that he had not allowed his wife to go off by herself tonight—and on similar nights. He thought of all the evenings he had spent away from her, working; and he regretted them. He thought wonderingly of his fierce ambition and of the direction his life had taken; he thought of the hours he'd spent by himself, filling the yellow sheet that had brought him out here. *Contents of the dead man's pockets,* he thought with sudden fierce anger, *a wasted life.*

He was simply not going to cling here till he slipped and fell; he told himself that now. There was one last thing he could try; he had been aware of it for some moments, refusing to think about it, but now he faced it. Kneeling here on the ledge, the finger tips of one hand pressed to the narrow strip of wood, he could, he knew, draw his other hand back a yard perhaps, fist clenched tight, doing it very slowly till he sensed the outer limit of balance, then, as hard as he was able from the distance, he could drive his fist forward against the glass. If it broke, his fist smashing through, he was safe; he might cut himself badly, and probably would, but with his arm inside the room, he would be secure. But if the glass did not break, the rebound, flinging his arm back, would topple him off the ledge. He was certain of that.

He tested his plan. The fingers of his left hand claw-like on the little stripping, he drew his other fist until his body began teetering backwards. But he had no leverage now—he could feel that there would be no force to his swing—and he moved his fist slowly forward till he rocked forward on his knees again and could sense that his swing would carry its greatest force. Glancing down, however, measuring the distance from his fist to the glass, he saw that it was less than two feet.

It occurred to him that he could raise his arm over his head, to bring it down against the glass. But, experimentally in slow motion, he knew it would be an awkward girl-like blow without the force of a driving punch, and not nearly enough to break the glass.

Facing the window, he had to drive a blow from the shoulder, he knew now, at a distance of less than two feet; and he did not know whether it would break through the heavy glass. It might; he could picture it happening, he could feel it in the nerves of his arm. And it might not; he could feel that, too—his fist striking this glass and being instantaneously flung back by the unbreaking pane, feel the fingers of his other hand breaking loose, nails scraping along the casing as he fell.

He waited, arm drawn back, fist balled, but in no hurry to strike; this pause, he knew, might be an extension of his life. And to live even a few seconds longer, he felt, even out here on this ledge in the night, was infinitely better than to die a moment earlier than he had to. His arm grew tired, and he brought it down and rested it.

Then he knew that it was time to make the attempt. He could not kneel here hesitating indefinitely till he lost all courage to act, waiting till he slipped off the ledge. Again he drew back his arm, knowing this time that he would not bring it down till he struck. His elbow protruding over Lexington Avenue far below, the fingers of his other hand pressed down bloodlessly tight against the narrow stripping, he waited, feeling the sick tenseness and terrible excitement building. It grew and swelled toward the moment of action, his nerves tautening. He thought of Clare—just a wordless, yearning thought—and then drew his arm back just a bit more, fist so tight his fingers pained him, and knowing he was going to do it. Then with full power, with every last scrap of strength he could bring to bear, he shot his arm forward towards the glass, and he said "Clare!"

He heard the sound, felt the blow, felt himself falling forward and his hand closed on the living-room curtains, the shards and fragments of glass showering onto the floor. And then, kneeling there on the ledge, an arm thrust into the room up to the shoulder, he began picking away the protruding slivers and great wedges of glass from the window frame, tossing them in onto the rug. And, as he grasped the edges of the empty window frame and climbed into his home, he was grinning in triumph.

He did not lie down on the floor or run through the apartment, as he had promised himself; even in the first few moments it seemed to him natural and normal that he should be where he was. He simply turned to his desk, pulled the crumpled yellow sheet from his pocket and laid it down where it had been, smoothing it out; then he absently laid a pencil across it to weight it down. He shook his head, wonderingly, and turned to walk towards the closet.

There he got out his topcoat and hat and, without waiting to put them on, opened the front door and stepped out, to go and find his wife. He turned to pull the door closed and the warm air from the hall rushed through the narrow opening again. As he saw the yellow paper, the pencil flying, scooped off the desk and, unimpeded by the glassless window, sail out into the night and out of his life, Tom Benecke burst into laughter and then closed the door behind him. ∾

APPETIZER

ROBERT ABEL

I'm fishing this beautiful stream in Alaska, catching salmon, char, and steelhead, when this bear lumbers out of the woods and down to the stream bank. He fixes me with this half-amused, half-curious look which says: You are meat.

The bear's eyes are brown, and his shiny golden fur is standing up in spikes, which shows me he has been fishing, too, perhaps where the stream curves behind the peninsula of woods he has just trudged through. He's not making any sound I can hear over the rumble of the water in the softball-sized rocks, but his presence is very loud.

I say "his" presence because temporarily I am not interested in or able to assess the creature's sex. I am looking at a head that is bigger around than my steering wheel, a pair of paws, awash in river bubbles, that could cover half my windshield. I am glad that I am wearing polarized fishing glasses so the bear cannot see the little teardrops of fear that have crept into the corner of my eyes. To assure him/her I am not the least bit intimidated, I make another cast.

Immediately I tie into a fat chinook. The splashing of the fish in the stream engages the bear's attention, but he/she registers this for the moment only by shifting his/her glance. I play the fish smartly, and when it comes gliding in, tired, pink-sided, glittering, and astonished, I pluck it out of the water by inserting a finger in its gill—something I normally wouldn't do in order not to injure the fish before I set it free, and I do exactly what you would do in the same situation—throw it to the bear.

The bear's eyes widen, and she—for I can see now, past her huge shoulder and powerful haunches, that she is a she—turns and pounces on the fish with such speed and nimbleness that I am numbed. There is no chance that I, in my insulated waders, am going to outrun her, dodge her blows, escape her jaws. While she is occupied devouring the fish—I can hear her teeth clacking together—I do what you or anyone else would do and cast again.

God answers my muttered prayer, and I am blessed with the strike of another fat salmon, like the others, on its way to spawning grounds upstream. I would like this fish to survive and release its eggs or sperm to perpetuate the salmon kingdom, but Ms. Bear has just licked her whiskers clean and has now moved knee-deep into the water and, to my

consternation, leans against me rather like a large and friendly dog, although her ears are at the level of my shoulder and her back is broader than that of any horse I have seen. Ms. Bear is intensely interested in the progress of the salmon toward us, and her head twists and twitches as the fish circles, darts, takes line away, shakes head, rolls over, leaps.

With a bear at your side, it is not the simplest thing to play a fish properly, but the presence of this huge animal, and especially her long snout, thick as my thigh, wonderfully concentrates the mind. She smells like the forest floor, like crushed moss and damp leaves, and she is as warm as a radiator back in my Massachusetts home, the thought of which floods me with a terrible nostalgia. Now I debate whether I should just drift the salmon in under the bear's nose and let her take it that way, but I'm afraid she will break off my fly and leader, and right now that fly—a Doctor Wilson number eight—is saving my life. So, with much anxiety, I pretend to take charge and bring the fish in on the side away from the bear, gill and quickly unhook it, turn away from the bear, and toss the fish behind me to the bank.

The bear wheels and clambers upon it at once, leaving a vortex of water pouring into the vacuum of the space she has left, which almost topples me. As her teeth snack away, I quickly and furtively regard my poor Doctor Wilson, which is fish-mauled now, bedraggled, almost unrecognizable. But the present emergency compels me to zing it out once again. I walk a few paces downstream, hoping the bear will remember an appointment or become distracted and I can sneak away.

But a few moments later she is leaning against me again, raptly watching the stream for any sign of a salmon splash. My luck holds; another fish smacks the withered Wilson, flings sunlight and water in silver jets as it dances its last dance. I implore the salmon's forgiveness: something I had once read revealed that this is the way of all primitive hunters, to take the life reluctantly and to pray for the victim's return. I think my prayer is as urgent as that of any Mashpee or Yoruban, or Tlingit or early Celt, for not only do I want the salmon to thrive forever, but I want a superabundance of them now, right now, to save my neck. I have an idea this hungry bear, bereft of fish, would waste little time in conducting any prayer ceremonies before she turned me into the main course my salmon were just the appetizer for. When I take up this fish, the bear practically rips it from my hand; and the sight of those teeth so close and the truly persuasive power of those muscled, pink-rimmed jaws cause a wave of fear in me so great that I nearly faint.

My vertigo subsides as Ms. Bear munches and destroys the salmon with hearty shakes of her head, and I sneak a few more paces downstream and rapidly also, with trembling fingers, tie on a new Doctor Wilson, observing the utmost care (as you would, too) in making my knots. I cast and stride downstream, wishing I could just plunge into the crystalline water and bowl away like a log. My hope and plan is to wade my way back to the narrow trail a few hundred yards ahead and, when Ms. Bear loses interest or is somehow distracted, make a heroic dash for my camper. I think of the thermos of hot coffee on the front seat, the six-pack of beer in the cooler, the thin rubber mattress with the blue sleeping bag adorning it, warm wool socks in a bag hanging

from a window crank, and almost burst into tears; these simple things, given the presence of Ms. Hungry Bear, seem so miraculous, so emblematic[1] of the life I love to live. I promise the gods—American, Indian, African, Oriental—that if I survive. I will never complain again, not even if my teenage children leave the caps off the toothpaste tubes or their bicycles in the driveway at home.

"Oh, home." I think, and cast again.

Ms. Bear rejoins me. You may or may not believe me, and perhaps after all it was only my imagination worked up by terror, but two things happened which gave me a particle of hope. The first was that Ms. Bear actually belched—quite noisily and unapologetically, too, like a rude uncle at a Christmas dinner. She showed no signs of having committed any impropriety, and yet it was clear to me that a belching bear is probably also a bear with a pretty-full belly. A few more salmon and perhaps Ms. Bear would wander off in search of a berry dessert.

Now the second thing she did, or that I imagined she did, was to begin—well, not *speaking* to me exactly, but *communicating* somehow. I know it sounds foolish, but if you were in my shoes—my waders, to be more precise—you might have learned bear talk pretty quickly, too. It's not as if the bear were speaking to me in complete sentences and English words, such as "Get me another fish, pal, or you're on the menu," but in a much more indirect and subtle way, almost in the way a stream talks through its bubbling and burbling and rattling of rocks and gurgling along.

Believe me. I listened intently, more with my mind than with my ears, as if the bear were telepathizing; and I know you're not going to believe this, but it's true—I am normally not what you would call an egomaniac with an inflated self-esteem such that I imagine that every bear which walks out of the woods falls in love with me, but I really did truly believe now that this Ms. Bear was expressing feelings of, well, *affection*. Really, I think she kinda liked me. True or not, the feeling made me less afraid. In fact, and I don't mean this in any erotic or perverse kind of way, but I had to admit, once my fear had passed, my feelings were kinda mutual. Like you might feel for an old pal or a dog. Or a favorite horse. I only wish she weren't such a big eater. I only wish she were not a carnivore, and I, carne.

Now she nudges me with her nose.

---

1 **emblematic:** symbolic.

"All right, all right," I say. "I'm doing the best I can."

Cast in the glide behind that big boulder, the bear telepathizes me. *There's a couple of whoppers in there.*

I do as I'm told, and wham! The bear is right! Instantly I'm tied into a granddaddy chinook, a really burly fellow who has no intention of lying down on anybody's platter beneath a blanket of lemon slices and scallion shoots, let alone make his last wiggle down a bear's gullet. Even the bear is excited and begins shifting weight from paw to paw, a little motion for her that nevertheless had big consequences for me as her body slams against my hip, then slams again.

Partly because I don't want to lose the fish, but partly also because I want to use the fish as an excuse to move closer to my getaway trail, I stumble downstream. This fish has my rod bent into an upside down U, and I'm hoping my quick-tied knots are also strong enough to take this salmon's lurching and his intelligent, broadside swinging into the river current—a very smart fish! Ordinarily I might take a long time with a fish like this, baby it in, but now I'm putting on as much pressure as I dare. When the salmon flips into the little side pool, the bear takes matters into her own hands, clambers over the rocks, pounces, nabs the salmon smartly behind the head, and lumbers immediately to the bank. My leader snaps at once, and while Ms. Bear attends to the destruction of the fish, I tie on another fly and make some shambling headway downstream. Yes, I worry about the hook still in the fish, but only because I do not want this bear to be irritated by anything. I want her to be replete and smug and doze off in the sun. I try to telepathize as much. Please, Bear, sleep.

Inevitably, the fishing slows down, but Ms. Bear does not seem to mind. Again she belches. Myself, I am getting quite a headache and know that I am fighting exhaustion. On a normal morning of humping along in waders over these slippery, softball-sized rocks, I would be tired in any case. The added emergency is foreclosing on my energy reserves. I even find myself getting a little angry, frustrated at least, and I marvel at the bear's persistence, her inexhaustible doggedness. And appetite. I catch fish; I toss them to her. At supermarket prices, I calculate she has eaten about six hundred dollars' worth of fish. The calculating gives me something to think about besides my fear.

At last I am immediately across from the opening to the trail which twines back through the woods to where my camper rests in the dapple shade of mighty pines. Still, five hundred yards separate me from this imagined haven. I entertain the notion perhaps someone else will come along and frighten the bear away, maybe someone with a dog or a gun; but I have already spent many days here without seeing another soul, and in fact have chosen to return here for that very reason. I have told myself for many years that I really do love nature, love being among the animals, am restored by wilderness adventure. Considering that right now I would like nothing better than to be nestled beside my wife in front of a blazing fire, this seems to be a sentiment in need of some revision.

Now, as if in answer to my speculations, the bear turns beside me, her rump pushing me into water deeper than I want to be in, where my footing is shaky, and she stares into the woods, ears forward. She has heard something I cannot hear or smell, and while I labor back to shallower water and surer footing, I hope some backpackers or some bear-poaching Indians are about to appear and send Ms. Bear a-galloping away. Automatically, I continue casting, but I also cannot help glancing over my shoulder in hopes of seeing what Ms. Bear sees. And in a moment I do.

It is another bear.

Unconsciously, I release a low moan, but my voice is lost in the guttural warning of Ms. Bear to the trespasser. The new arrival answers with a defiant cough. He—I believe it is a he—can afford to be defiant because he is half again as large as my companion. His fur seems longer and coarser, and though its substance is as golden as that of the bear beside me, the tips are black, and this dark surface ripples and undulates over his massive frame. His nostrils are flared, and he is staring with profound concentration at me.

Now I am truly confused and afraid. Would it be better to catch another salmon or not? I surely cannot provide for two of these beasts, and in any case Mister Bear does not seem the type to be distracted by or made friendly by any measly salmon tribute. His whole bearing—pardon the expression—tells me my intrusion into this bear world is a personal affront to his bear honor. Only Ms. Bear stands between us, and after all, whose side is she really on? By bear standards, I am sure a rather regal and handsome fellow has made his appearance. Why should the fur-covered heart of Ms. Bear go out to me? How much love can a few hundred dollars of salmon buy? Most likely, this couple even have a history, know and have known each other from other seasons, even though for the moment they prefer to pretend to regard each other as total strangers.

How disturbed I am is well illustrated by my next course of action. It is completely irrational, and I cannot account for it or why it saved me—if indeed it did. I cranked in my line and laid my rod across some rocks, then began the arduous process of pulling myself out of my waders while trying to balance myself on those awkward rocks in that fast water. I tipped and swayed as I tugged at my boots, pushed my waders down, my arms in the foaming, frigid water, then the waders also filling, making it even more difficult to pull my feet free.

I emerged like a nymph from a cocoon, wet and trembling. The bears regarded me with clear stupefaction, as if one of them had casually stepped out of his or her fur. I drained what water I could from the waders, then dropped my fly rod into them and held them before me. The rocks were brutal on my feet, but I marched toward the trail opening, lifting and dropping first one, then the other, leg of my waders as if I were operating a giant puppet. The water still in the waders gave each footfall an impressive authority, and I was half thinking that, well, if the big one attacks, maybe he'll be fooled into chomping the waders first and I'll at least now be able to run. I did not relish the idea of pounding down the trail in my nearly bare feet, but it was a better way to argue with the bear than being sucked from my waders like a snail from its shell. Would you have done differently?

Who knows what the bears thought, but I tried to make myself look as much as possible like a camel or some other extreme and inedible form of four-footedness as I plodded along the trail. The bears looked at each other, then at me as I clomped by, the water in the waders making an odd gurgling sound and me making an odd sound, too, on remembering just then how the Indians would, staring death in the eye, sing their death song. Having no such melody prepared and never having been anything but a bathtub singer, I chanted forth the only song I ever committed to memory: "Jingle Bells."

Yes, "Jingle Bells," I sang, "jingle all the way," and I lifted first one, then the other wader leg and dropped it, stomping down. "Oh what fun it is to ride in a one-horse open sleigh-ay!"

The exercise was to prove to me just how complicated and various is the nature of the bear. The male reared up, blotting out the sun, bellowed, then twisted on his haunches and crashed off into the woods. The female, head cocked in curiosity, followed at a slight distance, within what still might be called striking distance, whether I was out of my waders or not. Truly, I did not appreciate her persistence. Hauling the waders half full of water before me was trying work, and the superfluous thought struck me: suppose someone sees me now, plumping along like this, singing "Jingle Bells," a bear in attendance? Vanity, obviously, never sleeps. But as long as the bear kept her distance, I saw no reason to change my modus operandi.

When I came within about one hundred feet of my camper, its white cap gleaming like a remnant of spring snow and beckoning me, I risked everything, dropped the wader and sped for the cab. The bear broke into a trot, too, I was sure, because although I couldn't see her, had my sights locked on the gleaming handle to the pickup door, I sure enough could hear those big feet slapping the ground behind me in a heavy rhythm, a terrible and elemental beat that sang to me of my own frailty, fragile bones, and tender flesh. I plunged on like a madman, grabbed the camper door and hurled myself in.

I lay on the seat panting, curled like a child, shuddered when the bear slammed against the pickup's side. The bear pressed her nose to the window, then, curiously, unceremoniously licked the glass with her tongue. I know (and you know) she could have shattered the glass with a single blow, and I tried to imagine what I should do if indeed she resorted to this simple expedient. Fisherman that I am, I had nothing in the cab of the truck to defend myself with except a tire iron, and that not readily accessible behind the seat I was cowering on. My best defense, obviously, was to start the pickup and drive away.

Just as I sat up to the steering wheel and inserted the key, however, Ms. Bear slammed her big paws onto the hood and hoisted herself aboard. The pickup shuddered with the weight of her, and suddenly the windshield was full of her golden fur. I beeped the horn loud and long numerous times, but this had about the same effect as my singing, only caused her to shake her huge head, which vibrated the truck terribly. She stomped around on the hood and then lay down, back against the windshield which now appeared to have been covered by a huge shag rug.

Could I believe my eyes?

No, I could not believe my eyes. My truck was being smothered in bear. In a moment I also could not believe my ears, Ms. Bear had decided the camper hood was the perfect place for a nap, and she was snoring, snoring profoundly, her body twitching like a cat's. Finally, she had responded to my advice and desires, but at the most inappropriate time. I was trapped. Blinded by bear body!

My exhaustion had been doubled by the sprint for the camper, and now that I was not in such a desperate panic, I felt the cold of the water that had soaked my clothes, and I began to tremble. It also crossed my mind that perhaps Mister Bear was still in the vicinity, and if Ms. Bear was not smart enough or cruel enough to smash my window to get at me, he just might be.

Therefore, I started the engine—which disturbed Ms. Bear not a whit—and rolled down the window enough to stick my head out and see down the rocky, limb-strewn trail. I figured a few jolts in those ruts and Ms. Bear would be off like a shot.

This proved a smug assumption. Ms. Bear did indeed waken and bestir herself to a sitting position, a bit like an overgrown hood ornament, but quickly grew quite adept at balancing herself against the lurching and jolting of my truck, which, in fact, she seemed to enjoy. Just my luck. I growled, to find the first bear in Alaska who wanted to ride into town. I tried some quick braking and sharp-turn maneuvers I thought might send her tumbling off, but her bulk was so massive, her paws so artfully spread, that she was just too stable an entity. She wanted a ride, and there was nothing I could do about it.

When I came out of the woods to the gravel road known locally as the Dawson Artery, I had an inspiration. I didn't drive so fast that if Ms. Bear decided to clamber down, she would be hurt; but I did head for the main road which led to Buckville and the Buckville Cannery. Ms. Bear swayed happily along the whole ten miles to that intersection and seemed not to bat an eye when first one logging truck, then another, plummeted by. I pulled out onto the highway, and for the safety of both of us—those logging trucks have dubious brakes, and their drivers get paid by the trip—I had to accelerate considerably.

I couldn't see much of Ms. Bear except her back and rump, as I had to concentrate on the road, some of which is pretty curvy in that coastal area, shadowed also by the giant pines. But from the attitude expressed by her posture, I'd say she was having a whale, or should I say salmon, of a time. I saw a few cars and pickups veering out of the oncoming lane onto the shoulder as we swept by, but I didn't have time, really, to appreciate the astonishment of their drivers. In this way, my head out the window, Ms. Bear perched on the hood, I drove to the Buckville Cannery and turned into the long driveway.

Ms. Bear knew right away something good was ahead, for she rose on all fours now and stuck her nose straight out like a bird dog on a pheasant. Her legs quivered with nervous anticipation as we approached, and as soon as I came out of the trees into the parking area, she went over the front of the camper like someone plunging into a pool.

Don't tell me you would have done any differently. I stopped right there and watched Ms. Bear march right down between the rows of cars and right up the truck ramp into the cannery itself. She was not the least bit intimidated by all the noise of the machines and the grinders and stampers in there, or the shouting of the workers.

Now the Buckville Cannery isn't that big—I imagine about two dozen people work there on any given day—and, since it is so remote, has no hurricane fence around it and no security guard. After all, what's anybody going to steal out of there besides a few cases of canned salmon or some bags of frozen fish parts that will soon become some company's cat food? The main building is up on a little hill, and conveyors run down from there to the docks where the salmon boats pull in—the sea is another half mile away—and unload their catch.

I would say that in about three minutes after Ms. Bear walked into the cannery, twenty of the twenty-four workers were climbing out down the conveyors, dropping from open windows, or charging out of doors. The other four just hadn't got word of the event yet, but in a little while they came bounding out, too. They all assembled on the semicircular drive before the main office and had a union meeting of some vigor.

Myself, I was too tired to participate and in any case did not want to be held liable for the disturbance at the Buckville Cannery and so I made a U-turn and drove on to Buckville itself, where I took a room above the Buckville Tavern and had a hot shower and a really nice nap. That night in the Tap and Lounge, I got to hear many an exaggerated story about the she-bear who freeloaded off the cannery for a couple of hours before she was driven off by blowing, ironically enough, the lunch whistle loud and long. I didn't think it was the right time or place to testify to my part in that historical event, and for once kept my mouth shut. You don't like trouble any more than I do, and I'm sure you would have done about the same. ॐ

STAYING ALIVE

DAVID WAGONER

Staying alive in the woods is a matter of calming down
At first and deciding whether to wait for rescue,
Trusting to others,
Or simply to start walking and walking in one direction
Till you come out—or something happens to stop you.
By far the safer choice
Is to settle down where you are, and try to make a living
Off the land, camping near water, away from shadows.
Eat no white berries;
Spit out all bitterness. Shooting at anything
Means hiking further and further every day
To hunt survivors;

It may be best to learn what you have to learn without a gun,
Not killing but watching birds and animals go
In and out of shelter
At will. Following their example, build for a whole season:
Facing across the wind in your lean-to,
You may feel wilder,
And nothing, not even you, will have to stay in hiding.
If you have no matches, a stick and a fire-bow
Will keep you warmer,
Or the crystal of your watch, filled with water, held up to the
sun
Will do the same, in time. In case of snow,
Drifting toward winter,
Don't try to stay awake through the night, afraid of
freezing—
The bottom of your mind knows all about zero;
It will turn you over
And shake you till you waken. If you have trouble sleeping
Even in the best of weather, jumping to follow
The unidentifiable noises of the night and feeling
Bears and packs of wolves nuzzling your elbow,
Remember the trappers
Who treated them indifferently and were left alone.
If you hurt yourself, no one will comfort you
Or take your temperature,
So stumbling, wading, and climbing are as dangerous as
flying.
But if you decide, at last, you must break through
In spite of all danger,
Think of yourself by time and not by distance, counting
Wherever you're going by how long it takes you;
No other measure
Will bring you safe to nightfall. Follow no streams: they run
Under the ground or fall into wilder country.

Remember the stars
And moss when your mind runs into circles. If it should rain,
Or the fog should roll the horizon in around you,
Hold still for hours
Or days, if you must, or weeks, for seeing is believing
In the wilderness. And if you find a pathway,
Wheel rut, or fence wire,
Retrace it left or right—someone knew where he was going
Once upon a time, and you can follow
Hopefully, somewhere,
Just in case. There may even come, on some uncanny
evening,
A time when you're warm and dry, well fed, not thirsty,
Uninjured, without fear,
When nothing, either good or bad, is happening.
This is called staying alive. It's temporary.
What occurs after
Is doubtful. You must always be ready for something
to come bursting
Through the far edge of a clearing, running toward you,
Grinning from ear to ear
And hoarse with welcome. Or something crossing and
hovering
Overhead, as light as air, like a break in the sky,
Wondering what you are.
Here you are face to face with the problem of recognition.
Having no time to make smoke, too much to say,
You should have a mirror
With a tiny hole in the back for better aiming, for reflecting
Whatever disaster you can think of, to show
The way you suffer.

These body signals have universal meaning: If you are lying
Flat on your back with arms outstretched behind you,
You say you require
Emergency treatment; if you are standing erect and holding
Arms horizontal, you mean you are not ready;
If you hold them over
Your head, you want to be picked up. Three of anything
Is a sign of distress. Afterward, if you see
No ropes, no ladders,
No maps or messages falling, no searchlights or trails blazing,
Then chances are, you should be prepared to burrow
Deep for a deep winter.

Responding to Cluster Two

After Surviving?

Thinking Skill GENERALIZING

1. Compare what is important to Tom Benecke in "Contents of the Dead Man's Pockets" before and after his experience on the ledge.

2. Authors often use detailed literary **description** to help the reader become involved in the story. Select a descriptive passage from one of the pieces in this cluster that caused you to empathize with, or understand, a character. Be prepared to explain your choice.

3. Both Tom in "Contents of the Dead Man's Pockets" and the narrator in "Appetizer" used humor to help cope with danger. Describe a time when you or someone else used humor to cope with a difficult situation.

4. In the poem "Staying Alive," David Wagoner makes the following general statement: "Staying alive in the woods is a matter of calming down." What general statements—or **generalizations**—would the other characters in this cluster make about surviving difficult situations? You might complete the following sentences to help your thinking:

    Staying alive on a ledge is a matter of . . .

    Surviving a visit from a bear is a matter of . . .

Writing Activity: Reacting to a Survival Situation

Select one of the situations below. Then describe what you would do to survive for two months. Finally, write a **generalization** about survival based on your description.

- You are alone in the Canadian wilderness with the following items: a hatchet, a knife, a piece of string, a paperclip, a beeper, two books, pencils and pens, a water bottle, one sandwich in a plastic bag, two candy bars, a parka, and your backpack. You have no way to contact the outside world.

- You are living in the 1850s—a time without television, telephones, radio, indoor plumbing, electricity, computers, video games, cars, or grocery stores.

- You are on a new planet in another solar system without a spaceship (yours is broken). There is no way to contact Earth, and you have very little knowledge about the plants and animals on the planet.

Generalizing involves

- recognizing particular elements in a situation
- seeing common elements in dissimilar situations
- applying lessons to other situations
- creating an overall statement to define a situation

CLUSTER THREE

WHAT WOULD YOU RISK?

Thinking Skill   EVALUATING

BATTLE BY
THE BREADFRUIT TREE

THEODORE WALDECK

Smith and I were anxious to procure motion pictures of a herd of baboons. We had tried and tried, with no success whatever, though we saw many of these creatures. Our camp was some miles from a little ravine through which a little stream ran. Beyond the ravine was a plateau leading back to thick woods. The baboons, scores of them, came out of these woods with their young to play on the plateau, to drink from the stream, and to fight for the favors of the females. Often Smith and I watched them, tried to photograph them, but could never get close enough. The baboons enjoyed what we were doing. They thought it was a game of some sort.

Once we set up the camera at the edge of the plateau in order to take them when they came through the woods at dawn to greet the sun. We didn't even come close, for when the baboons saw us, they charged like a shrieking army of savages. They threw sticks and stones at us, and we fled as though the devil and all his imps were at our heels. A grown bull baboon could have torn either of us to shreds. We didn't even stop to take our camera. We felt sure that our camera would be a wreck when we returned, which could not be until the baboons had retired from the plateau. We went back then, to find it exactly as we had left it. They had not so much as touched it.

"We must get those pictures," said Smith, "and I think I know the answer. Those breadfruit trees this side of the ravine. That big one, with the leafy top . . ."

"Yes?"

"We go there now and build a platform, up among the leaves, set up our camera, take blankets, a thermos bottle filled with hot tea, and spend the night. Then, when they come out in the morning, we'll be looking right down on them."

I saw that he was right, and we set about it. The trekkers got boards from the camp and carried them to the tree. Big limbs were cut off and lashed high among the leaves at the top of the breadfruit tree. Then the boards were laid across the limbs, the camera set up. We had supper, took our blankets, and went to the tree to spend an uncomfortable night; but however uncomfortable it might be, it would not matter if we got our pictures.

Night. We sat hunched up with our blankets over us listening to the sounds of the night. Now and again we dozed off. I'd have a cigarette; Smith would smoke a pipe. Then we'd waken. The wind blew steadily toward us from the plateau, which we could see dimly in the moonlight. The hours wore on.

Finally, animals began to greet the growing morning, though it would be some time, if they stuck to schedule, before the baboons appeared. I sat back on my blanket now—it was already warm enough to do without it—and watched the day break. I never tired of doing that. The sun comes up in a different way in Africa. First the leaves would be black. Then a grayish haze would outline their shapes. Then the gray would lighten into the green of the leaves. Then the sun itself would strike through, and morning would be with us, covering that part of Africa with a mixture of colors that ran through all the spectrum. Sunlight played upon colors like a mighty organist upon the keys, and the keys were everything the sunlight touched; when the dawn was come, it was music made visible. Not just the music that men played, but the music of Nature herself, with all the sounds that Nature used. A great sword of crimson was like a blood-curdling scream you could not hear because you came before it sounded or after the sound had passed—and the sword struck deeply into the ravine and raised itself to slash across the plateau on which the baboons usually played. The green of the trees was light and like a touch of agony somehow—not the agony of pain, but the agony of an unexplainable kind of ecstasy. Far away and all around were the mounded hills, with the veldt between them, and some of the hills wore caps of crimson or orange or gold, and some were still touched with the mystery of distance or the night that had not yet left them. Whatever color or combination of colors you cared to mention, you could find there. And they came out of the east in a magical rush, like paint of all colors flung across the world by a painter bigger than all the earth itself.

I sighed and drank it in. Smith was looking out through the leaves, watching for the baboons to appear. Then he nudged me, and I made an end, for the moment, of dreaming. I parted the leaves in utter silence, making sure that my lens was uncovered and aimed at the plateau, and looked through. The baboon herd had not come, but a single baboon and her baby. Smith had not actually seen her coming. One moment he had been watching, seeing nothing. Then he had blinked his eyes, and she was there. He signaled me to start the camera. I noted that the wind was toward us. I felt sure that the rest of the baboons would come, following this one. The mother baboon, while her baby played across the plateau behind her, came down to its edge to peer into the ravine, perhaps to dash down for a drink. I started the camera. It was almost silent but not quite. And with the first whirring sound, which we ourselves could scarcely hear, though we were right beside it, the mother jumped up and looked around. Her ears had caught the little sound. She looked in all directions, twisting her head swiftly, and even in this her eyes kept darting to her young one. I stilled the whirring. We did not move or make a sound, even a whisper. She was so close we could see her nose wrinkling as she tried to get our scent. But the wind was toward us, and she got nothing. She even looked several times at the breadfruit tree that hid us.

I was about to start grinding again when a terrific squall came from the baby. It caught at my heart, that sound. I know it caught the heart of Smith, too, for I could see it in his face. The mother baboon whirled around, so fast one could scarcely see the movement. The baby was jumping swiftly to the top of a rock, which was all too low to be of any use to him, as protection against the creature that was close behind him.

That creature was a hunting leopard, and it, like the baboon, had come so softly and silently that we had not seen it. It was simply there, a murderous streak behind the baby baboon. Did the female hesitate for a single moment? Not at all. If the leopard were a streak, so was the mother baboon. She shot toward the leopard and was in the air above him, reaching for his neck, while he was in midleap behind the baby, which now sat upon the rock and uttered doleful screams of terror.

The great cat instantly had his work cut out for him. For the baboon, by gripping his neck from behind, beyond reach of those talons, could break it. And that was what she tried, with hands and feet and killing incisors. But while I knew nothing of this fighting combination, the leopard must have, for he did what any cat would instinctively do in such a case. He spun to his back and reached for the baboon with all four of his brutally armed paws. One stroke across the abdomen of the baboon, and she would be killed outright. But she knew something of leopards.

Smith did not make a sound, nor did I. I don't think we even breathed. The great cat recovered himself as the baboon jumped free of the leopard and ran toward her baby. The leopard charged the baboon. The baboon waited until the last minute, shot into the air, allowed the cat to go under her, turned in the air, and dropped back for the killing hold on the back of the neck again.

She got some hair in her mouth, which she spat out disgustedly. The baby kept on squalling. As nearly as I could tell—though I probably would not have heard even the trumpeting of elephants or the roaring of lions—there was no sound other than the screaming of the female baboon, the squalling of her baby, and the spitting and snarling of the leopard.

This time, when the leopard whirled to his back to dislodge the baboon, he managed to sink his claws into the baboon. I saw the blood spurt from the baboon's body, dyeing her fur. I knew that the smell of blood would drive the leopard mad, and it did. He would just as soon eat the meat of a grown baboon if he could not have the baby.

Both stood off for a second, regarding each other, to spit out fur and hair. Then the leopard charged once more. Again the baboon leaped high, started down, reaching for that neck. And this time, when she came down, the leopard had already turned, and she could not entirely avoid landing among those fearful talons. Even a baboon could not jump from a spot in midair. For a brief moment there was a terrific flurry of infighting, from which came the snarling of the leopard, the screaming of the she-baboon. Now we could see the leopard, not the baboon, the latter trying with all her strength and agility to escape a disemboweling stroke from one of the four feet of the killer. Then both were so mixed up, and fighting so much all over the plateau, that we could not distinguish them, We could tell they were together because they formed a ball of fighting fury, and the sounds of the two animals came out of the pinwheel of murderous action.

How long it lasted I do not know. To the she-baboon and her baby it must have seemed ages. It may have been seconds, even a minute. And then they were standing off, catching their breath, spitting out fur, regarding each other again. Both were tired. To my utter amazement the baboon was holding her own with the leopard. At that moment I would not have known which one had the edge, if either. For both were panting, weary, and stained with blood.

Neither gave ground. By common consent they stood for a few seconds, the baboon on her hind legs, the leopard crouching on all fours. Then the leopard charged. Again the baboon went into the air to let the leopard go under her. She knew better, at this stage of the game, than to run away or jump to either side. The leopard could overtake her if she ran, could turn instantly and follow her if she jumped to either side. So up and over was her only chance. Again she came down. But this time she was expecting the cat to whip upon his back and present his talons, and was ready. She twisted aside a little, and to the front, perhaps with some idea of reaching for the neck from the underside, now uppermost. The forepaws of the leopard lashed at her. The sun gleamed on the exposed talons and showed that they were red with baboon blood. I could see long weals across the abdomen of the baboon. She had evaded those slashes at the last moment, each time. Feeling the talons' touch she had got away, just enough to escape disemboweling, not enough to escape deep, parallel gashes that reached inward for her life.

Now I began to see how the fight was going to go, though neither Smith nor I could have done anything about it because we were spellbound, rooted to our place in the breadfruit tree, watching something that few explorers had ever seen: a battle between a leopard and a baboon! And for the best reason in the world—the baboon to protect her baby.

But now the she-baboon was tiring. It was obvious in all her movements, though I knew and the leopard knew that as long as she stood upright and could see him, she was dynamite—fury incarnate, capable of slaying if she got in the blows she wanted. So far she had not made it.

Now she panted more than the leopard did. She did not entirely evade his rushes, though she jumped over him as before. But she did not go as high or twist as quickly in the air. She couldn't. Her body was beginning to weigh too much for her tiring muscles. She was like an arm-weary prizefighter who has almost fought himself out. But her little eyes still glared in defiance, her screaming still informed him that she was ready for more. Now there were other slashes upon her face, her head, her chest, and her abdomen—clear down even to her hands and feet.

She was a bloody mess. But she never even thought of quitting. They drew apart once more, spitting fur. They glared at each other. Several times I saw the orange eyes of the leopard, and there was hell in them— the hell of hate and fury and thwarted hunger.

Now he charged before the baboon had rested enough. He was getting stronger, the baboon weaker. His second wind came sooner perhaps, and he sorely needed it. Even yet the baboon could break his neck, given the one chance.

Again the baboon went into the air, came down, and was caught in the midst of those four paws. Again the battle raged, the two animals all mixed up together, all over the plateau. The little one squalled from his boulder, and there was despair in his voice. He cried hopeless encouragement to his mother. She heard, I knew she did, and tried to find some reserve with which to meet the attacks of the killer.

That last piece of infighting lasted almost too long. There was no relief from it, and the nerves of the two men who watched were strained to the breaking point, though neither was aware of it. How long they had held their breath they did not know.

The two beasts broke apart, and I saw instantly that the leopard had at last succeeded, managing the stroke he had been trying for since the battle began. He had raked deeply into the abdomen of the baboon. The result may be well imagined. The baboon drew off slowly and looked down at herself. What she saw told her the truth—that even if the leopard turned and ran away this minute, she was done.

But did she expect mercy? Death did not grant mercy in Africa—certainly not on this particular morning.

The baboon noted the direction of the leopard's glance. The great cat was crouched well back but facing the rock on which the baby squalled. He licked his chops, looked at the dying she-baboon, and growled, and it was as though he said:

"Not much time now. And when you are gone, nothing will keep me from getting him!"

As if the leopard had actually screamed those words, I got the thought which raced through his evil head. And the baboon got it too. For she turned slowly, like a dead thing walking, and moved to turn her back toward the rock, so that the baby was almost over her head.

Then she looked at the leopard once more and screamed as though she answered: "Perhaps, but over my dead body!"

The leopard charged again, for the last time. It would be easy now. And as the she-baboon set herself against that last charge, the strangest, most nearly human cry I ever heard went keening out across the veldt. It bounced against the breadfruit trees, dipped into the ravine; it went back through the forest whence the other baboons usually came to play and drink. It went out in all directions, that cry, across the plain. It rolled across the mounded hills. It was a cry that could never be forgotten by those that heard it.

And then, in the midst of the cry—like none she had uttered while the fight had been so fierce—the leopard struck her down. She sprawled, beaten to a pulp, at the base of the boulder, while that last cry of hers still moved across the veldt.

And now, sure that the she-baboon was dead, the leopard backed away, crouched, lifted his eyes to the baby on the rock.

I came to life then, realizing for the first time what I was seeing. I couldn't have moved before. But now, somehow, my rifle was in my hands, at my shoulder, and I was getting the leopard in my sights. Why had I not done it before, saved the life of the mother? I'll never know. Certainly, and sincerely, I had not allowed the fight to continue simply in order to see which would win out. I had simply become a statue, possessing only eyes and ears.

I got the leopard in my sights as he crouched to spring. I had his head for a target. I'd get him before he moved, before he sprang. The baby—looking down, sorrow in his cries, with a knowledge of doom too—had nowhere to go. I tightened the trigger. And then . . .

On the instant, the leopard was blotted out, and for several seconds I could not understand what had happened, what the mother's last cry had meant. But now I did. For living baboons, leaping, screaming, had appeared out of nowhere. They came, the whole herd of them, and the leopard was invisible in their midst. I did not even hear the leopard snarl and spit. I heard nothing save the baboons, saw nothing save the big blur of their bodies, over and around the spot where I had last seen the leopard.

How long that lasted I do not know. But when it was over, another she-baboon jumped to the rock, gathered up the baby, and was gone. After her trailed all the other baboons. Smith and I looked at each other, and if my face was as white and shocked as his, it was white and shocked indeed. Without a word, because we both understood, we slipped down from the tree, crossed the ravine, climbed its far side, crossed the plateau, looked down at the dead she-baboon, then looked away again. One mother had fought to the death for the life of her baby and had saved that life. We looked around for the leopard who had slain her. We couldn't find a piece of it as big as an average man's hand! So the baboons had rallied to the dying cry of the mother baboon.

We went slowly back to the tree, got our camera down, returned with it to our camp. Not until we were back did we realize that neither of us, from the beginning of that fight to its grim and savage end, had thought of the camera, much less touched it.

One of the greatest fights any explorer ever saw was unrecorded. ᶜᵛ

THE MAN IN THE WATER

ROGER ROSENBLATT

On January 13, 1982, Air Florida Flight 90 plowed into the 14th Street
Bridge in Washington D.C. and plunged into the frigid waters of
the Potomac River. The plane hit seven vehicles, killing four motorists and
74 passengers. Only six people survived. This is one passenger's story.

As disasters go, this one was terrible but not unique, certainly not among the worst on the roster of U.S. air crashes. There was the unusual element of the bridge, of course, and the fact that the plane clipped it at a moment of high traffic, one routine thus intersecting another and disrupting both. Then, too, there was the location of the event. Washington, the city of form and regulations, turned chaotic, deregulated, by a blast of real winter and a single slap of metal on metal. The jets from Washington National Airport that normally swoop around the presidential monuments like famished gulls are, for the moment, emblemized by the one that fell; so there is that detail. And there was the aesthetic clash as well—blue-and-green Air Florida, the name a flying garden, sunk down among gray chunks in a black river. All that was worth noticing, to be sure. Still, there was nothing very special in any of it, except death, which, while always special, does not necessarily bring millions to tears or to attention. Why, then, the shock here?

Perhaps because the nation saw in this disaster something more than a mechanical failure. Perhaps because people saw in it no failure at all, but rather something successful about their makeup. Here, after all, were

Passengers are rescued from the waters of the Potomac.

EDITORIAL ESSAY **85**

two forms of nature in collision: the elements and human character. Last Wednesday, the elements, indifferent as ever, brought down Flight 90. And on that same afternoon, human nature—groping and flailing in mysteries of its own—rose to the occasion.

Of the four acknowledged heroes of the event, three are able to account for their behavior. Donald Usher and Eugene Windsor, a park police helicopter team, risked their lives every time they dipped the skids into the water to pick off survivors. On television, side by side in bright blue jumpsuits, they described their courage as all in the line of duty. Lenny Skutnick, a 28-year-old employee of the Congressional Budget Office, said: "It's something I never thought I would do"—referring to his jumping into the water to drag an injured woman to shore. Skutnik added that "somebody had to go in the water," delivering every hero's line that is no less admirable for its repetitions. In fact, nobody had to go into the water. That somebody actually did so is part of the reason this particular tragedy sticks in the mind.

But the person most responsible for the emotional impact of the disaster is the one known at first simply as "the man in the water." (Balding, probably in his 50s, an extravagant mustache.) He was seen clinging with five other survivors to the tail section of the airplane. This man was described by Usher and Windsor as appearing alert and in control. Every time they lowered a lifeline and floating ring to him, he passed it on to another of the passengers. "In a mass casualty, you'll find people like him," said Windsor, "But I've never seen one with that commitment." When the helicopter came back for him the man had gone under. His selflessness was one reason the story held national attention; his anonymity another. The fact that he went unidentified invested him with a universal character. For a while he was Everyman, and thus proof (as if one needed it) that no man is ordinary.

Still, he could never have imagined such a capacity in himself. Only minutes before his character was tested, he was sitting in the ordinary plane among the ordinary passengers, dutifully listening to the stewardess telling him to fasten his seat belt and saying something about the "no smoking sign." So our man relaxed with the others, some of whom would owe their lives to him. Perhaps he started to read, or to doze, or to regret some harsh remark made in the office that morning. Then suddenly he knew that the trip would not be ordinary. Like every other person on that flight, he was desperate to live, which makes his final act so stunning.

For at some moment in the water he must have realized that he would not live if he continued to hand over the rope and ring to others. He *had* to know it, no matter how gradual the effect of the cold. In his judgment he had no choice. When the helicopter took off with what was to be the last survivor, he watched everything in the world move away from him, and he deliberately let it happen.

Yet there was something else about the man that kept our thoughts on him and which keeps our thoughts on him still. He was *there,* in the essential, classic circumstance. Man in nature. The man in the water. For its part, nature cared nothing about the five passengers. Our man, on the other hand, cared totally. So the timeless battle commenced in the Potomac. For as long as that man could last, they went at each other, nature and man: the one making no distinctions of good and evil, acting on no principles, offering no lifelines; the other acting wholly on distinctions, principles and, one supposes, on faith.

Since it was he who lost the fight, we ought to come again to the conclusion that people are powerless in the world. In reality, we believe the reverse, and it takes the act of the man in the water to remind us of our true feelings in this matter. It is not to say that everyone would have acted as he did or as Usher, Windsor and Skutnik. Yet whatever moved these men to challenge death on behalf of their fellows is not peculiar to them. Everyone feels the possibility in himself. That is the abiding wonder of the story. That is why we would not let go of it. If the man in the water gave a lifeline to the people gasping for survival, he was likewise giving a lifeline to those who observed him.

The odd thing is that we do not even really believe that the man in the water lost his fight. "Everything in Nature contains all the powers of Nature," said Emerson. Exactly. So the man in the water had his own natural powers. He could not make ice storms or freeze the water until it froze the blood. But he could hand life over to a stranger, and that is a power of nature too. The man in the water pitted himself against an implacable, impersonal enemy; he fought it with charity; and he held it to a standoff. He was the best we can do. ❧

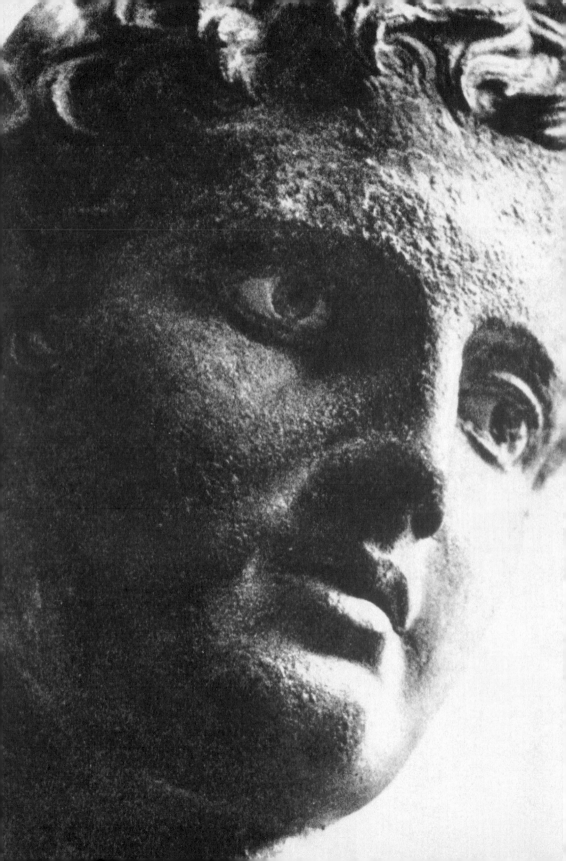

JARED

DAVID GIFALDI

Early for his appointment, Jared walked the paved trail beside the converted house that was the clinic. Normally the parklike setting with its bank of alders and tiny creek below helped him to relax before going in. But today even the playful antics of a pair of ducks couldn't take his mind off the slip of paper in his pocket. He wished Ryan hadn't given him the paper . . . hadn't clapped him on the back and said, "She's all yours," with that knowing wink. Ryan was supposed to be his friend. You'd think the big jerk would know better. Know that the mere thought of meeting girls made Jared feel as if he were hanging from some window ledge—forty stories up—fingers already starting their slide.

"Ryan," he breathed, his face beginning to throb with the pain that was always just below the surface now. Reaching up, he doffed the floppy-brimmed felt hat that had become his protection from the eyes of the world and wiped the wet from his forehead. He was at the place where the path became dirt, curving to the footbridge that led to the apartments across the way. He didn't hear the woman and the little girl who rounded the curve together. His eyes met the woman's for only an instant before veering down to the girl's. He could see the girl's lips . . . how they'd already begun to shape themselves into a *Hello*. Then stopped. He turned as abruptly, jamming the hat back on and looking to where the ducks were spinning and bobbing like well-oiled wind-up toys. Behind him he could hear the woman's soft hushing. Footsteps moving away with increased speed. The little girl's voice was all the louder for the quiet of the trees.

"But, Mommy, what happened to that boy's face?"

▲   ▲   ▲

The waiting room was set up to be calming. Framed landscapes on the walls, classical music . . . a thick, cushiony, blue carpet. The reception-ist's name was Beth, an older college student with a ready smile who always looked at Jared straight on.

"Hi, kid," Beth said, looking up from a textbook. "How's it going? Don will be a few minutes yet. Need a cup of java?"

"Naw. I think I'll go it alone this time."

He hadn't meant to be funny, but Beth cracked up. Jared had to admit it felt good to hear her snorty laugh. He took a seat in the corner near a plant that was almost a tree and picked up a *New Yorker*. Thumbing the pages, he was aware of the paper still stuffed in his pocket, wondering if he would share it with Don or chicken out.

He'd gotten through a half-dozen cartoons, none of which were that great, when the fat woman who preceded him every Tuesday suddenly sailed in from the hall. Usually the woman came out red-eyed and clutch-ing a fistful of tissues. But today she was tissueless and beaming. Sometimes it was that way for Jared, too. When a session went particu-larly well, he'd come out feeling light as a fluff ball . . . like one of those dandelion things you chased as a kid. The feeling would last for as long as he could keep from looking into a window or seeing his reflection in a mirror. Two or three days if he was extra careful.

"Hi, Jared," Don called from the doorway. "Be just a sec. Go ahead back."

Soft murmurs issued from the closed doors along the hall. Jared walked to the end, entered Don's office, and threw himself into the over-stuffed chair by the window. Don came in a moment later, tall and gray-haired—a cup of coffee in hand—and closed the door behind him before taking the leather chair opposite. Setting the coffee on the side table, he checked his calendar book, folded his glasses into their case, eyed the little clock only he could see, and leaned back, giving Jared the look that said, *Ready when you are.*

This was the hard part . . . starting. Sometimes whole clumps of time would go by with Jared staring out the window or tracing the intricate designs of the oriental rug with his eyes. Don never began the sessions. It must be what he learned in Shrink School . . . something about letting the patient make the first move. Jared thought it was a bunch of bull. He hated that initial silence during which he felt like a laboratory specimen, severed and laid out, his every move and expression open for study.

"I've never seen you without your hat."

Jared jerked alert, thinking it impossible that Don had spoken first. "What?"

"I said, you've been coming here twice a week for almost three months now, and I've never seen you without your hat."

Jared tugged the hat even lower over the right side of his face. He knew he could leave. Get up, say good-bye, and be gone. Don had always said there were no rules. He could hop the bus and get home early . . . throw something together for dinner before his mom got home. Or walk. He liked walking now that it was getting darker earlier. Liked the dark.

"There's this girl," he said suddenly, surprised to hear the urgency in his voice. His gaze swept the room, leaping over Don, before skidding to a stop on the rug. He had his right thumb hooked in the pocket of his jeans, fingers moving over the paper within.

"I don't know her or anything. I mean, I know her name and I've seen her once, but I don't know her. Ryan met her at the mall. She was with some friends . . . girls. They all go to Franklin, the next school over. And Ryan and Jeff and Mark introduced themselves. I was—around. You know . . . I didn't want to blow their chances. So I stayed out of sight and watched to see if the guys scored."

"Scored?"

"Not in that way. To see if the girls would give them the time of day . . . if they were interested."

"And were they?"

"Yeah. They did a lot of gabbing and got on real good. Even had Cokes together at Friendly's. You could tell they were having a good time—" His voice cracked, so he cut it off.

"And how did that make you feel?"

Don's standard line. Jared pictured a building collapsing and Don being the first on the scene, moving from corpse to corpse: *How did that make you feel? . . . How did that make you feel?*

"I felt awful. I mean, I felt okay at first, seeing as how Ryan and the guys were scoring. Then I felt awful."

Jared's left eye had already learned to compensate for the right, which had been narrowed and pulled askew by the last surgery. His left now traced the bars of color in the rug, following the staircase design . . . down, over, down, over. There were shapes and patterns in everything, he thought. Even the spaces between shapes were shapes if you looked hard enough. He'd found a whole zoo of animals in the hospital ceiling after the accident. It was a textured ceiling. Textured, bumpy surfaces were best for finding things. Surfaces discolored and scarred and sewn together. Just that morning he'd found the Big Dipper in the mirror while brushing his teeth. Each star a white blotch on a raw, pink picket sky. He wondered if the doctors played the shape game during the skin grafts. Using his face for a game board.

Don's eyes remained steady and expressionless. Jared squirmed, slouching lower and flinging his leg over the chair's armrest.

"You see, this one girl . . . Megan . . . the one Ryan hit it off with . . . She was beautiful. Not in the magazine way or anything. But really sharp." He shook his head. "It's hard to explain . . . the way she . . . you know . . . walked, moved. She smiled a lot, too. Only the smiles were real, not like some girls. I could just tell she was nice. Really nice. Not just cute-and-cool nice. But *really* nice. And afterward Ryan said she was. Said I'd really like her. And—"

He stopped, knowing he'd reached that familiar place of self-pity. He could feel the warm, black ooze trying to suck him under.

"Why weren't you with the boys?" Don said. "They're your friends, aren't they?"

Jared set his jaw. "You know why I wasn't with them. They were trying to impress girls. To score. They didn't need someone tagging along who would scare the girls away or make them sick."

"So you decided you'd only be a negative in this affair."

"Not just a negative. I'd blow the whole thing."

"I see. So you let the others introduce themselves and they had a good time and you stayed off by yourself, mad as hell. And that's it?"

"What do you mean, is that it?"

"Well, it doesn't sound much different from how you usually react to meeting new people."

"It's different! Because—" He yanked the paper from his pocket. "Because later on they all traded phone numbers, and today Ryan said it was too bad in a way that he and Stephanie were getting back together because he had that phone number of the girl at the mall. Megan. The nice one. The one I'd asked him about. And he gave it to me. Gave me the number."

He felt like an idiot holding his fist up in the air like that, his heart racing and his breath coming hard, as if he were about to lead some troops into battle. Lowering his hand, he shoved the paper back in his pocket.

"Are you gonna call?"

Sometimes Jared thought he could make a better therapist than Don. Don could be so thick. "What kind of a question is that?" he asked.

"Just a question. Are you?"

"Am I *what*?"

"Gonna call this girl . . . this Megan?"

"No!"

"Because you're afraid she might . . . what?"

"Because if I call and say you don't know me but I think you're nice and could we go out sometime and she says yes—what then?"

"You could go out?"

"And scare her to death when she opens the door?"

"How many people have died from looking at you?"

It wasn't even worth answering. Died? . . . None. Sure. But how many had been repulsed? How many had looked away or stared with wrinkled faces like it was painful to see? One little boy had even screamed. Screamed right there in the library where he'd been playing under Jared's table. The kid had popped up, giggling, his little teeth suddenly slicing into his lip before letting go with a scream that brought half a dozen people racing over.

"I'm a creature feature," Jared spat. "A regular Phantom of the Opera. An elephant man."

"You're nothing of the sort," Don said. "You're scarred. From an accident. You were burned. And the marks are there. But it's getting better. You'll have more surgery. You'll . . ."

But of course Jared had heard it all before, and he closed himself off. Sealed himself into a box of silence. The same box he closed around himself in school or at home when his mind threw up the white flag of surrender, pleading for respite from the hell of mirrors and murmurs and pitying expressions. Inside the box the walls were smooth and dark and comforting—the air warm and fluid and only slightly fetid. He stayed there in the safe and the dark and the quiet. Until Don's voice came through like a shoulder-nudging wake-up call: "I'm afraid our time is up for today. We'll see you next time."

▲   ▲   ▲

It was one of those hurried dinners—toasted cheese sandwiches and canned lentil soup. Picking up on Jared's mood, his mother waited till they were finished before asking about the session.

"I'm tired of going," Jared said. "Twice a week for how long? It's a waste of money. You could save yourself a bundle. I want to quit anyway." He cleared off their plates and slid them noisily into the sink.

"You can't quit," she said. "You promised you'd give it six months. It was part of the deal."

Jared scoffed, but he knew it was true. It had been his idea to move. His mother's company had an office in Salem, and she had agreed to apply for a transfer only if Jared promised to enter therapy. At the time he was sick of his old classmates and friends offering their gloomy expressions of pity while keeping a safe distance away, as if he had some contagious disease. He thought a clean break would be good. He was sorry now. It was even worse being both a freak *and* a stranger. Having no history. He wanted to put a sign around his neck. *Hi, my name is Jared Wheatley. I wasn't born this way. I even thought I was someone once. Liked baseball and girls and even school sometimes . . . believed I was slick and smart and the rest of it. But that was before the nightmare. Before a ball of fire ate up half my face.*

If a person was still interested, he could turn the sign over, sweeten their curiosity with some real gore: *How, you want to know? Excuse me for smiling. It was a barbecue. That's right. A good old-fashioned barbecue. A cookout. Ever hear of a sixteen-year-old knocking over a can of gas into a fire? . . . Trying to save a plate of stupid hot dogs from tipping and elbowing over a can of gas he should never have been using anyway? Ever smelled your own skin burning? Felt your face sliding from side to side? But I go on. Here, give me your hand. Glad to meet you.*

His hand moved outward and he brought it back quickly, embarrassed that his daydreams were becoming so real. It would be something to discuss with Don. Right up his alley. Fantasy versus reality. Jared saw the look of sadness in his mother's eyes, the look that said, *I know how it is.* But she couldn't. How could she? "I'm going upstairs," he said, hurrying past her.

In his room the music, the homework, nothing could take his mind off the paper with Megan's number. On the bus ride home he'd taken the paper from his pocket and smoothed it some before slipping it into his geometry book. Now he took it out, placing it on the desk before him, intrigued by the bold letters, the purple ink, the way the sevens in the number were crossed European style so that they looked like *f*s.

The phone was in plain sight. On the dresser across from him. A sleek, black number with a green-lit dial pad. His mother had bought it for him after the move to encourage him to be more social. The phone was another waste of money as far as Jared was concerned. The only person he ever called was Ryan, and him hardly at all since they lived so close. Not that there was a whole lot to talk about even with Ryan. The two hadn't even a single class together at school. Ryan had befriended Jared because they were neighbors. One of Jared's worst fears was that Ryan had been instructed by his parents to be nice to the new freak down the street.

He left the desk lamp on low and flicked off the overhead so the room would be darker. The dresser's mirror was mostly covered with posters and magazine pics—action shots of cars, baseball players, skiers, and board sailors. A small square of mirror had been left uncovered—too high to see into without standing on your toes. A bit of insurance against accidentally scaring himself.

"Megan."

He let the name drop off his lips, watching his mouth move, his tongue curl. He stood on tiptoes, his left side facing the glass, amazed at how perfect that side was. He said the name again, trying for just the right stress. The music coming from the radio had suddenly softened. A ballad of some sort. Soft and intimate, like he imagined Megan's voice would be.

The ringing drummed deep in his ear. He wondered when he had picked up the phone. How he had pressed the numbers so quickly. Was he nuts? Put the damned thing down before—

"Hello."

And again. "Hello."

A girl's voice. He cleared his throat. "Megan?"

"Yes, who's calling, please?"

He paced to the center of the room and had to dive back to catch the phone before it toppled off the dresser.

"This is Jared . . . Jared Wheatley . . . You don't know me."

There was a pause. Then, "Hey, is this a prank call? Or one of those obscene things?"

"NO . . . This is a good call . . . I mean, I'm a friend of Ryan's."

"Do I know a Ryan?" She said it almost to herself and Jared could see her brow furrowing beneath her thick bangs, a finger poised at her lips.

"You met him at the mall in front of Friendly's the other day . . . Saturday."

"Oh, yeah . . . How come this isn't him then?"

The heat shot from his neck to his face, needle points of pain flashing on and off. "Because Ryan isn't available," he said. "I mean, see, he's going steady with somebody and—"

"And you're his friend and he gave you my number, thinking I was up for grabs by whoever happened to have the ability to dial? Get a life, Jared whatever-your-name-is . . . I'm not for sale *or* hire."

"Don't! Don't hang up! It's not like that. I mean, Ryan's a good guy. He wouldn't think of anyone like that."

"But you would."

"No, I just saw you with him and—"

"You were one of the other guys?"

"No, I was . . ." *Hiding.* "Working . . . working at the restaurant . . . behind the counter."

"Do you lie often?"

"Huh?"

"I wasn't born yesterday. You've got lie written all over your voice."

"Listen," he said, pressing now, scared. "I just called to say hi and to say I think you're . . ." *Neat—no, that's sick.* "I mean, I thought you were . . ." *Beautiful?—too much.*

He felt like a four-year-old on the verge of tears. "Megan, I'm sorry. It was all a mistake. Good-bye."

Crumpling the paper, he flung it hard against the wall. *You're a dork,* he told himself. *A first-class freak of a dork.*

▲   ▲   ▲

The box of silence stayed tight and tamperproof throughout the next day. He was a nonentity, a ghost floating to and from classes. After school he walked until the cold November night settled in, forcing him home. It was the hanging up that upset him the most. Such a coward's way.

After dinner he retreated to his room. Made a stab at completing some homework. Actually got halfway through a play that had been assigned for English before realizing he had no idea what the play was about. Frantic, he searched until he found the paper wrapped in dust, stuck behind the leg of his desk. Tearing the ball open, he lunged for the dresser, finger flying over the green-lit pad before his mind had a chance to say no.

"Megan?"

"Are you the same kid from last night?"

His tongue refused to move.

"I thought you might call back."

"You did?"

"Yeah, you sounded desperate."

"Oh, I'm not desperate . . . Just wanted to be friends."

"With a perfect stranger?"

"I'm sorry for last night . . . I mean, for hanging up. I don't usually act—"

"Let's hope not," she cut in. "It's Jared, right?"

"Yes."

"You wanna talk? Is that why you called again?"

"Please." It sounded wheedling and he wanted to take it back, but she gave him no time.

"Might not be a bad idea," she said. "My parents are glued to the tube and I'm bored stiff since they never let me out midterm week. I guess even if you are an ax murderer, you can't do much damage over the phone. Go ahead, shoot."

▲　▲　▲

"We talked for over an hour!" Jared told Don the next day.

"I still can't believe it. School, parents, likes, hates, sports . . . you name it. It was so easy!

"It's perfect, don't you see," he added. "We can be friends over the phone. She said to call again tonight. She likes to take things real slow when it comes to boy-girl stuff. I told her I was the same. It's perfect."

"You should be proud of yourself," Don said. "For taking the plunge. Look at what you would have missed."

It was true, Jared thought. For the first time in so long he felt free. Wondrously, gloriously free. Later over dinner his mother asked who he'd been talking to the previous night. "It was past eleven when I turned off the light and you were still yapping away."

"Mom, I can't talk about it yet. I mean, it's good. But I'm a little nervous about it. You won't feel bad if I play this one close to my chest for a while, will you?"

"Play it however you like. I'm just glad to see you so happy. You seem like a new person. Like the person—

"No," she said. "That's not what I mean. You're just fine with me, up or down . . . any old way. I just want the best for you." Her eyes were moist. "You've been through a lot."

Jared turned away, afraid that he might get teary, too. His mother had stuck with him through all of it. He knew it was joy she was feeling now, but tears were tears and he didn't want to start blubbering. You start crying, and you never know where it might lead . . . might lead right back to the unanswerable. Questions like *Why me?* and *How could such a thing happen?*

"Your hair is growing out some," she said.

Jared's hand swung up to touch the stubs over his right ear. The doctors had said it was still too early to tell if the follicles there had been overly damaged by the fire. He thought he'd noticed the bristles moving out some, but was afraid it might just be wishful thinking.

"You really think so?"

"I know so," she said. "Here, let me see."

But he couldn't bring himself to let her touch him. He felt naked enough having to reveal his ugliness to her every day from a distance. He couldn't stomach the thought of having her really look, up close like that. It wasn't only his vanity. It was also that he knew how much she hurt for him, and he didn't want her to hurt. So he made a face, crinkling up his nose, and asked if she was wearing a new perfume.

"Same old stuff," she said, smiling.

He nodded. "Always liked that one."

▲ ▲ ▲

Friday night. Saturday night. Sunday. Monday. Tuesday. Wednesday. Jared called each night at ten. He and Megan were so good together. There was never a lack of things to talk about. The only subject off limits for Jared was the accident. And anything to do with his looks. Megan tried to press him on the looks issue only once, but it was clear from the way he suddenly clammed up that he didn't want to talk about it, and she let it go. "It's even better this way," she said. "I can picture you any way I want."

"So when are you going to ask her out?" Don asked on Thursday.

"We haven't talked about it. She seems to like it this way, too. She likes to take thing slow. She's shy. I told you that." There was a tremor in his voice and his stomach went queasy. "I mean, sooner or later, sure, we'll have to meet. But she doesn't appear to be in a hurry and —"

"And you still haven't discussed the accident?"

"Why do you have to ruin everything?" Jared shot.

"Am I ruining everything?"

"What if I don't want to meet her? What if we're both happy just the way it is? I think you should just stay out of it."

"Even if I think you might be making a mistake?"

"You always said there are no mistakes. Just opportunities for learning and all that. Now you're telling me I'm making a mistake."

"I just think it's best to be honest."

"Yeah, well, you don't know everything. Things are fine, okay? Just fine."

And they were, Jared's nightly phone calls sometimes stretching until midnight. The two of them . . . exploring, discovering, teasing, flirting, laughing. Until week three. Friday. A note of impishness to Megan's voice. "What size shoe do you wear?"

"What?"

She giggled. "What's your shoe size?"

He couldn't help a giggle himself. Her sunny way was always infectious with him. "Eight and a half, I guess. Why?"

" 'Cause I'm putting together a composite."

"A what?"

"A composite . . . of you. I figure if you give me your shoe size, waist and inseam measurements, neck and pecs and head . . . then I'll be able to figure out what you look like."

"Forget the numbers," he said. "I can describe it all in three words— tall, dark, handsome."

"Mmmm," she said. "But my reception must be off. I can't tell if you're fibbing or not."

"Mom always said I was cute as a button," he said. "Does that help?"

"Nope, moms don't count. Godzilla thought her baby was cute, too."

He felt suddenly nauseous, his gaze pitching from desk to bed to floor, desperate to locate a new topic.

"If you must know, I'm dying with curiosity over the whole thing," Megan said. "I mean, I probably know you better than any boy I've known in a long time. But my mental image keeps fuzzing up . . . changing. Won't it be exciting to meet?"

"Sure."

"Sure." She mimicked the lackluster tone of his voice. "You don't sound excited at all."

"No, I am. I mean, it'd be great to really meet you. It's just that I thought we could maybe hold off for a while longer."

"Why?"

"Because—"

"See. No reason whatsoever. That settles it then. We can meet tomorrow. At the mall. Afternoon would be best, then it wouldn't be like a heavy thing . . . you know, no pressure-filled Saturday-night thing. We could just meet in front of Friendly's and have a Coke or something. Sound good?"

"Yeah . . . sure . . . except I think tomorrow is when Mom wanted me to—"

"Uh-uh," she said. "My antennae are working loud and clear now. I told you I could spot a lie a mile off. Your social calendar is about as full as mine for tomorrow. Which translates to *free*. Nope. It's tomorrow, all right. How's two sound to you?"

His insides felt raked.

"Good," she said when he didn't answer.

They talked some more. Or rather, Megan did. Jared had to hang on the best he could. He hadn't planned on this. Hadn't planned on it at all. He wished now he'd taken the possibility more seriously with Don. Don would tell him everything would be all right. It was another of Don's standard lines. He could use a standard line right then. Something familiar. Something known—like that TV jingle he liked so much. The one he'd sung to himself in the hospital when the pain tore at him. No words. Just a tune. On TV the music was accompanied by pictures of trees and mountain trails. *La-la-laaa . . . la-laa-la.*

"I guess you're just not in a talkative mood tonight," Megan said, finally.

"Not really."

"Well, we'll have plenty of time tomorrow. See you then, my mysterious friend."

▲ ▲ ▲

He lay in bed, humming the *la-la* tune, trying to stop his stomach from whirling. His face was hot, the heat pricking its way down to his neck and chest. When the sweat came, he tore off the covers and lay naked except for his shorts. He couldn't figure out why he was thinking of his dad. His dad who had left so suddenly when Jared was only ten. Even years later,

Jared had had a hard time bringing himself to go down to the basement of the old house alone. The basement had been his dad's domain. It was where they had built things together. Where they'd set up Jared's train set . . . an American Flyer with forty feet of figure-eight track complete with tunnels, bridges, and a water tower that stood over a foot high. He wondered now if he had ever really forgiven his dad for dropping dead like that. Dead at the age of thirty-seven. People said it was unheard of. Didn't happen to a healthy young man with a wife and a son and everything to live for.

Wearily, he got up, stumbled out to the hall . . . made his way to the bathroom, where he fell to his knees over the toilet and purged the snakes from his stomach.

"Jared?"

"It's okay, Mom. Go back to bed."

"Are you sick?"

"No. Go back to bed."

"Take a pain pill if you need it."

"I'm all right."

He rinsed his mouth and swallowed a capful of Listerine, letting his eyes focus on the face in the mirror. On the three rectangular slabs of skin sewn one below the other. They looked like farm fields seen from a plane far above—fields tied together with barbed wire and cut by irrigation streams flashing gray and purple and white.

Slamming the light switch, he returned to bed. The wringing in his stomach had stopped. And he slept, dreaming of himself as a young boy. Seeing himself running and laughing and calling out to his cousins behind his grandmother's barn. "Ready or not," he could hear himself saying. And he went out looking for them, only to discover they were running away . . . farther and farther from him. They weren't hiding at all. Just running. Looking back with frightened faces. He ran till he could run no longer, then dropped to the ground, crying out for them to stop, crying for his father to stop them from running, yelling how unfair it was as the dream took a turn . . . The young boy suddenly transformed to that of one older. Himself at sixteen. Shrieking. Stumbling. Arms flailing. His mother sobbing as she cradles his toweled head in her hands. The hurt like nothing he has ever experienced. So that he must hum. Hum the *la-la* jingle. Wonder where his father is as his mother rocks him in the pulsing, stench-filled dark of the towel.

▲   ▲   ▲

It was past eleven the next morning when he woke. After showering from the neck down, he washed his hair in the sink and daubed at his face with the special towelettes that smelled of menthol. Pulling on a clean pair of jeans, he spent a good ten minutes deciding on a shirt, choosing in the end his light blue pinstripe, freshly pressed. Gently, he fingered some cream onto his face, a cosmetic that dulled the streaks of color and paled the lumpy ridges. Or was supposed to. He didn't check long enough to make an assessment . . . just looked to see he hadn't left any gobs.

Downstairs he poured himself a cup of coffee, slurping it quickly while telling his mother he needed to pick up a few things at the mall.

"I'll be leaving soon, myself," she said. "I've got a million little errands to run . . . I could drop you off if you want."

"No," he replied much too loudly. "I mean, thanks, but I want to walk."

On the way the wind stung coldly and he turned up his jacket collar and lowered the brim of his hat, quickening his pace even though he knew he was early. He wondered if Megan was as nervous as he . . . if she'd taken extra care in deciding what to wear . . . if her parents knew about their meeting . . . if she'd swallowed that tall, dark, and handsome line. It didn't matter. He probably wouldn't go through with it anyway. Didn't have to. He could back out anytime. Breeze right past her. A stranger. Cool and anonymous.

Once inside the mall he headed to the sunken area of benches down from Friendly's. It was from here that he had watched Ryan and Megan and the others the first time. The benches were laid out to look like a maze. About eight benches in all, with vinyl cushions and tiled backs. He chose the bench in the middle, farthest from the walkways on either side. Here he sat, hunkered into his jacket, his hat angled low over his face, eyeing the currents of shoppers, his gaze darting regularly to the restaurant.

He gasped audibly when he saw her exit one of the smaller boutiques. Stopping to check the time, she slung the colorful canvas carryall higher over her shoulder before crossing to the restaurant with the somewhat embarrassed look of one who knows she may be being watched. Still, she looked confident. And beautiful. More beautiful than he had remembered. He got a kick over the fact that she was wearing her dad's Chicago Cubs jacket, the one she'd talked about. The jacket swung open as she walked, revealing a classy Western shirt with silver tips on the collar and big silver buttons. Reaching Friendly's she turned, eyes sweeping the mallway in either direction.

Jared froze up. He was a block of ice sitting there on the bench, only his mind working. He had no right, he thought. No right to put her in this kind of a situation. Don was right. He should have been honest with her from the beginning. It wasn't fair to have someone get to know you . . . for you to draw someone into liking you without telling them your biggest flaw. His mind swerved back to Don. What was it Don had told him so often? To go with his gut? But his gut said to run. Was that it? Was that what he was feeling? Yes. Scared. Scared, pure and simple.

He saw Megan check the hanging clock above. Watched her smile when she saw a little girl try to play hopscotch on the large marble floor tiles . . . the smile giving way to a look of disapproval when the girl's mother yelled and yanked the child back, causing the girl to break into a soft cry.

Reined in, Jared thought. Whenever something good happens, there's always someone or some god-awful thing that happens that pulls you back. Snuffing out what was good. Leaving sadness and resentment and pain. So that you have to find a way to go on. Find a place where there are no surprises . . . no more hurts. He wondered if the little girl was finding a way even then. Her crying had stopped, her tiny face suddenly hard as stone as her mother whisked her past the benches. Was she building a box? Making a place where the yanks and the scorn and the put-downs could never enter?

Abruptly, he got up. Megan would have to discover for herself what a creep he was. Someone who would make a date and then cop out. A creep. Better a creep, he thought, than to be discovered with his face put together with slabs of skin from his nether parts. *Forget it,* he said to himself.

He was a fish swimming upstream against the rush of incoming shoppers, taking one last look at her before reaching the door. In the vestibule beyond the inner doors was a crowd of young people, laughing and talking. Jared felt their stares when he pushed open one of the doors. Heard their conversation dwindle to almost nothing. It wasn't just the smoky air and the closed-in feeling that make him retch . . . made him turn and throw his shoulder into the glass, the door bursting open so that he was back inside, nearly bowling over a group of exiting shoppers in his rush for the wall. It was his gut. Speaking so loud it almost picked him off his feet. Saying, *No, no, no!*—the same as it had when the fireball hit.

Spinning on his heels, he ran into two women loaded down with shopping bags . . . mumbled an excuse . . . went quickly on, his stomach in knots, heart fluttering like some chained bird under his shirt. He knew it now. How it was the box that his gut was crying out against. The box . . . with its sour air and aloneness and dark. His gut like a prisoner wrongly accused, saying *no* to the silence . . . the shame . . . the invisible oblivion of the box.

Megan was looking the other way when he came up to her. Looking for him. For Jared. The voice over the phone. The child running and laughing and playing. The boy. The almost man. The kernel that was Jared and would always be.

Pulling off his hat with one hand, he flicked his hair with the other. "Megan?"

She turned quickly.

The initial look of delight and anticipation would be forever engraved in his mind.

"It's me," he said, leading with his gut. "Jared." ❧

PLAINSWOMAN

WILLIAMS FORREST

The cold of the fall was sweeping over the plains, and Nora's husband, Rolf, and his men had ridden off on the roundup. She was left on the ranch with Pleny, a handyman, who was to do the chores and lessen her fears.

Her pregnancy told her that she should hurry back East before the solemn grip of winter fell on the land. She was afraid to have the child touch her within, acknowledge its presence, when the long, deep world below the mountains closed in and no exit was available—for the body and for the spirit.

Her baby had not yet wakened, but soon it would. But gusts of wind and a forbidding iron shadow on the hills told her that the greatest brutality of this ranch world was about to start. And then one morning Pleny came in for his breakfast, holding the long finger of his left hand in the fingers of his right. For some time he had concealed his left hand from her, holding it down or in his pocket; and from the way he had held himself, she thought it was a part of his chivalry, his wish to have table manners, use his right hand and sit up straight with a lady. But now he held it before him like a trophy, and one he did not wish to present.

Nora had been thinking of New England when Pleny came in—of the piano and the gentle darkness of her mother's eyes, of frost on the small windowpanes, and the hearth fires, of holidays and the swish of sleighs, of men with businesslike faces and women who drank tea and read poetry, of deep, substantial beds and the way the hills and the sea prescribed an area, making it intimate, and the way the towns folded into the hills. She was thinking of home and comfort, and then Pleny walked in; the dust trailed around his ankles, and the smell of cattle seemed to cling to his boots. A thousand miles of cattle and plains and work and hurt were clung like webs in his face.

Nora had made eggs, ham, bread and coffee for the breakfast, but Pleny made them objects of disgust as he extended his hand, as shyly but as definitely as a New England lad asking for a dance, and said, "I got the mortification,[1] ma'am. I have to let you see it."

She looked at his index finger and saw the mortification of the flesh, the gangrene. He held the finger pointed forward, his other fingers closed. He pressed the finger with his other hand, and the darkened skin made a crackling sound like that of ancient paper or dangerous ice over a pond. And above the finger some yellow streaks were like arrows pointing to the hairs and veins above his wrist.

Nora smelled the food, gulped, stood up and turned away.

"I got to come to you, ma'am," said Pleny. "I finally got to come to you."

He spoke firmly but shyly, but she did not hear his tone; she heard only his demand. And her emotion rejected it and any part of it. Her emotion said that he should not have come to her and that she had nothing to do with it, and would not and could not. She walked toward the fireplace, staring into the low flames. She heard the wind coax the sides of the house. She said, pretending nothing else had been mentioned, "Pleny, there's your breakfast." She itemized it, as if the words could barricade her against him. "Eggs . . . ham . . . bread . . . hot coffee—hot coffee."

But after she had spoken she heard nothing but his steady, waiting breathing behind her. And she understood that she would have to turn and face it. She knew he was not going away and would not happily sit down to eat and would not release her.

The fire spoke and had no answer, even though it was soft. She turned and saw the weather on Pleny's face, the diamonds of raised flesh, the scars. And she knew that death was in his finger and was moving up his arm and would take all of him finally, as fully as a bullet or freezing or drowning.

"What do you expect of me, Pleny?" she said.

He moved with a crinkling hard sound of stained dungarees, hardened boots and his dried, reluctant nature. "Ma'am," he said, "I don't

---

1 **mortification:** gangrene; rotting body tissue when the blood supply is cut off because of injury or disease.

want you to think I'm a coward. I just wouldn't want you to get that notion. I'll take my bumps, burns and cuts, just like I did with this finger on the lamp in the bunkhouse and then on the gate before it could heal. I'll take it without complaining, but I sure don't like to doctor myself." His lake-blue eyes were narrowed with thought, and the erosion in his face was drawn together, as if wind and sun were drawing his face closer together, the way they did the land in the drought. "I just can't bear to cut on myself," he said, lowering his head with a dry shame. He lifted his head suddenly and said, "I suppose I'd do it out on the plain, in the mountains, alone. But I can't do it here."

His Adam's apple wobbled as he sought in his throat for words. His lips were cracked and did not easily use explanations. "It just seems sinful, ma'am," he said, "for a man to hack on himself." Suddenly his eyes were filled with burning knowledge. He spoke reasonably, without pleading, but an authority was in his voice. "Ma'am, you never saw a man do that, did you, when somebody else was around to doctor him?"

She had watched and listened to his explanation without a stirring in her; she had done so as if she were mesmerized, like a chicken before a snake. Gradually his meaning penetrated her and told her what he meant.

"Ma'am," he said, "would you do me the kindness to take off this here finger?"

She ran senseless, as if she were attempting to run long, far, back to New England. The best she could do was run through the rooms of the haphazardly laid-out house and get to her room and close the door and lean against it. She was panting, and her eyes were closed, and her heart was beating so hard that it hurt her chest. Slowly she began to feel the hurts on her shoulders, where she had struck herself against the walls and doors. Rolf had started this house with one room and had made rooms and halls leading off from it as time went on. She had careered[2] through the halls to her room as if fighting obstacles.

She went to her bed but did not allow herself to fall down on it. That would be too much weakness. She sat on the edge of the bed, with her hands on her lap. Her wish to escape from this place was more intense than ever within her. And her reasons for it ran through her brain like a cattle stampede, raising acrid dust and death and injury—and fear, most of all.

2 **careered:** moved at top speed.

Her fear had begun in the first frontier hotel in which she had spent a night. Rolf had been bringing her west from New England to his ranch in the springtime. The first part of the ride on the railroad had been a pure delight. Rolf's hand was big, brown, with stiff red hairs on the back, a fierce, comforting hand; and her own had lain within it as softly as

Bridge Street,
Helena, Montana, 1860's.

a trusting bird. The railroad car had had deep seats and decor that would have done credit to a fine home. As those parts of the world she had never seen went past, mountain, stream and hamlet, she had felt serene: and the sense of adventure touched her heart like the wings of a butterfly. She was ready to laugh at each little thing, and she had a persistent wish to kiss Rolf on the cheek, although she resisted such an unseemly act in front of other people.

"I know I'll be happy," she said. And his big, quiet hand around hers gave her the feeling of a fine, strong, loving secure world.

But the world changed. After a time they were on a rough train that ran among hills and plains, and after a while there was nothing to see but an endless space with spring lying flat on it in small, colorful flowers and with small, bleak towns in erratic spaces, and the men on the train laughed roughly and smelled of whisky. Some men rode on the roof of the car and kicked their heels, fired guns and sang to a wild accordion.

Rolf's hand seemed smaller. His tight, strong, burned face that she had so much admired seemed remote; he was becoming a stranger, and she was becoming alone with herself. She, her love for him, her wish for adventure, were so small, it seemed, in comparison to the spaces and the crudity.

One night the train stopped at a wayside station, and the passengers poured out as if Indians were attacking. They assailed the dining room of the canvas-and-board hotel as if frenzied with starvation. In the dining room Rolf abruptly became a kind of man she had never known. He grabbed and speared at plates like any of the others and smiled gently at her after he had secured a plateload of food for her that made her stomach turn. After affectionately touching her hand, he fought heartily with the others to get an immense plateload for himself. Then he winked at her and started to eat, in the same ferocious way as the others. His manners in New England had seemed earthy, interesting, and powerful—a tender animal. But here, here he was one more animal.

That night they shared a bedroom with five other people, one a woman who carried a pistol. Rolf had bought sleeping boards and blankets so that they would not have to share beds with anyone. The gun-carrying woman coughed and then said, "Good night, all you no-good rascals."

Rolf laughed.

The spring air flipped the canvas walls. The building groaned with flimsiness and people. Nora had never before heard the sounds of a lot of sleeping people. She put her face against Rolf's chest and pulled his arm over her other ear.

Late at night she woke crying. Or was she crying? There was crying within her, and there were tears on her face. But when she opened her eyes, the night was around her, without roof or walls, but there was the water of rain on her cheeks. Rolf bent over her. "We're outside," he said.

"You were suffering. Exhausted, suffering, and you spoke out loud in your sleep."

"Why did you bring me out here?" The blankets were wet, but she felt cozy. He was strong against her. The night was wet but sweet after the flapping, moaning hotel.

Some water fell from his face to hers. Was Rolf crying? No, not Rolf, no. But when he spoke, his voice was sad. "I told you how it would be, didn't I?"

"I didn't know," she said. "I didn't know how awful it could be."

He spoke powerfully but troubledly. "I can't always take you outside, away from things. I can't do that. There'll be times when I can't do for you, when only you can do it yourself."

"Don't be disturbed," she said, holding him closer. "Don't be disturbed." The smell of the wet air was sweet, and it was spring, and they were alone and small again in an enclosed world made of them both, and she was unafraid again. "I'll be all right," she promised. "Rolf, I will be all right."

▲ ▲ ▲

She slept with that promise, but it did not last through the next day. The train stopped after noontime in the midst of the plain. Cattle ran from the train. A lone horseman rode toward them out of curiosity. The sky was burning. Some flowers beside the tracks lifted a faint gossamer odor. Men were drinking and making tea on the stove of the car. Then they all were told that a woman two cars ahead was going to have a child now. Nora was asked to go forward to attend her.

The impressions of the next few hours had smitten her ever since. The car in which the woman lay on a board suspended between seats across the aisle was empty except for herself and the third woman on the train. The cars before and after this one had also been emptied. The woman helping her said that the men were not even supposed to hear the cries of the woman in labor. It would not be proper. But were the men proper anyway? From the sounds in the distance, Nora could tell they were shouting, singing and shooting, and maybe fighting and certainly drinking.

She had seen labor before, when the doctor was unavailable, blocked away by snow, so she was good enough here, and there were no complications. But there was no bedroom with comforters, a fire and gentle women about. The woman helping her was the one who wore a pistol, and she cussed.

When the child, a boy, was born, the gun-toting woman shouted the word out the window, and the air was rent with shouts and shooting. The woman on the board lifted her wet head, holding her blanketed baby. "A boy to be a man," she said. "A boy to be a man." She laughed, tears streaming from her eyes.

The woman with the gun said softly, "God rest Himself. A child of the plains been born right here and now."

The train started up. Nora sat limply beside the mother and child. Men walked into the car, looked down and smiled.

"Now, that's a sight of a boy."

"Thank you kindly," said the woman.

"Now ma'am, that boy going to be a cattleman?" said another.

"Nothing else."

"Hope we wasn't hoorawing too much, ma'am," said a tall man.

"Jus' like my son was born Fourth of July. Thank you kindly."

"Just made this tea, but it ain't strong's should be," said a man carrying a big cup.

"Thank you kindly."

Another man came up timidly—strange for him; he was huge. It turned out he was the husband. He did not even touch his wife. He looked grimly at his son. The woman looked up at him. "All these folks been right interested," he said.

The woman smiled. The train jerked and pulled. Her face paled. The man put his hand on her forehead. "Now, just don't fret," he said. "Just don't fret."

"Thank you kindly," she said.

In her own seat, next to Rolf, Nora was pale. She flinched when the train racketed over the road. Rolf gripped her hand.

"Rolf?"

"Yes, honey?"

"She's all right. The woman with the baby—she's all right."

"I know."

"Then be quiet, don't be disturbed. I can tell from your hand. You're disturbed."

He looked out the window at the plains, at the spring. "The trip took longer than I thought," he said. "It's time for spring roundup. I ought to be at the ranch."

She was shocked. This great, terrible, beautiful thing had happened, and he was thinking of the roundup. Her hand did not feel small and preserved in his; it felt crushed, even though his fingers were not tightly closed.

"Rolf?" Her shock was low and hurt and it told in her voice. "Rolf. That woman had a baby on the train. It could have been awful. And all you can think of now is the roundup."

He looked around at the others in the car. Then he lowered decorum a little and put his arm around her.

He whispered, "Honey, I tried to tell you—I tried. Didn't you listen? On the plains we do what has to be done. Why, honey, that woman's all right, and now we've got to get to roundup."

"But can't we—can't we be human beings?" she said.

He held her. "We are, honey," he said. "We are. We're the kind of human beings that can live here."

She remembered all that, and she remembered also that within two days after they had got to the ranch, Rolf had gone out with the men on spring roundup. That time, too, Pleny had been left with her to take care of the home ranch. She had been sad, and he had spoken to her about it in a roundabout fashion at supper one night. Pleny ate with her in the big kitchen when the others were gone, instead of in the bunkhouse. And he was shy about it but carried a dignity on his shyness.

"Don't suppose you know that the cattle're more important than anything out here?" he said.

"It seems I have to know it," said Nora.

Pleny was eating peas with a knife. She had heard about it but had never been sure it was possible.

"Couldn't live here without the cattle," he said.

"It seems to me that living here would be a lot better if people thought more about people."

"Do. That's why cattle's more important."

"I fail to understand you."

Pleny worked on steak meat. "Ma'am, cattle's money, and money's bread. Not jus' steak, but bread, living. Why, ma'am, if a man out here wants a wife, he has to have cattle first. Can't make out well enough to have a wife and kids without you have cattle."

"I don't think it's right," she had said then in the springtime. "I don't think it's right that it should be that way."

And Pleny had replied, "Don't suppose you're wrong, ma'am. I really don't." He wiped his mouth on his sleeve. "Only trouble is, that's the way it is here, if you want to stay."

She hadn't wanted to stay. As soon as she was sure she was pregnant, she wanted to go home. The spring had passed, and the summer hung heavy over the plains. The earth, the sky, the cattle, the people had dry mouths, and the dogs panted with tongues gone gray. The wind touched the edges of the windmills, and water came from the deep parts of the earth, but you could not bathe in it. The water was golden and rationed, and coffee sometimes became a luxury—not because you didn't have the coffee, but because the cool, watery heart of the earth did not wish to serve you.

The fall roundup time came; and just before the outfit moved out, a cowboy, barely seventeen years old, had broken his leg. Rolf had pulled the leg straight, strapped a board to it, and put the boy on a horse with a bag of provisions. "Tie an extra horse to him," Rolf had commanded Pleny, "in case something happens."

Pleny had done so. Rolf had asked the boy, "Got your money?"

"Got it right here."

"Now, you get to that doctor."

"Sure enough try."

"Now, when you're fixed up," said Rolf, "you come back."

"Sure enough will."

Nora knew that it would take eight to ten days for the boy to get to the nearest doctor. She ran toward the boy and the horses. She held the reins and turned on Rolf. "How can you let him go alone? How? How?"

Rolf's face had been genial as he talked to the boy, but now it hardened. But the boy, through a dead-white pain in his face, laughed. "Ma'am," he said, "now who's going to do my work and that other man's?"

"Rolf?" she said.

Rolf turned to her, took her hands. "Nora, there isn't anybody that can go with him. He knows that."

The boy laughed. "Mr. Rolf," he said, "when I get my own spread, I'm going to go out East there to get a tender woman. I swear." He spurred with his good leg and, still laughing, flashed off into dust with his two horses.

"Rolf? He might die."

Rolf bowed his head, then fiercely lifted it. "Give him more credit."

"But you can't—" she began.

"We can!" he said. Then he softened. "Nora, I don't know what to say. Here—here there's famine, drought, blizzard, locusts. Here—here we have to know what we must do if we want to stay."

"I don't like it," she said.

A wind lifted and moved around them, stirring grass and dust. In the wind was the herald of the fall—and therefore the primary messenger of the bitter winter. In the wind was the dusty harbinger of work, of the fall roundup.

"Soon I'll have to go," he said, "for the roundup."

"I know."

"The plains are mean," he said. "I know. I came here and found it. But I—I don't hate it. I feel—I feel a—a bigness. I see—I see rough prettiness." He bowed his head. "That isn't all I mean." He looked at her. "Soon I have to go. You'll be all right. Pleny will take care of you."

She hadn't told him that she was sure she had a child within her. She felt that she must keep her secret from this wild place because, even if it were only spoken, the elements might ride like a stampede against her, hurting her and her child, even as they did in the dark when she was alone and the wind yelled against the walls beside her bed and told her how savage was the place of the world in which she lived.

There was a knock on her door. She looked up. Her hands, folded in her lap, gripped each other. She did not answer.

"Ma'am?"

She said nothing.

"It's Pleny. I just can't sit down and eat, ma'am, worrying about this mortification of the flesh I got. I just can't sit down to anything like that. I just have to do something."

She made her hands relax in her lap.

"I have it wrapped up in my kerchief ma'am," said Pleny, "but that ain't going to do it no good."

She closed her eyes, but opened them at once, staring at the door.

Pleny said, "I ain't going to leave you and the ranch, ma'am. Couldn't do that. I have my chores to do."

A small, unbidden tear touched the edge of her eye and slipped down.

There was a silence, and then he said quietly, "The doc's so far away, don't 'spect I could get there before the mortification took more of my flesh. Sure would hate that. Sure would hate that."

A second tear burned silver on the edge of her eye and dropped and burned golden down her cheek and became acid on her line of chin, and her wrist came up and brushed it away.

She heard the wind and many messages and she imagined Pleny waiting. She felt a sense of response, of obligation, of angry maternal love, as if all the wistful hope and female passion of her nature had been fused, struck into life, made able because she was woman and was here, and birth, survival, help, lay potent, sweet, powerful in her heart and in her hands.

She stood up. "Pleny?'

"Yes, ma'am?"

"What must I do?"

He was silent, and she opened the door. Angrily, then firmly, she said, "Let's go outside, Pleny."

"Yes, ma'am."

She held the kindling ax. Pleny had his finger on the block. He closed his eyes. The wind pulled her skirts. She looked up for a moment at the whirling light. Then, in necessity and tenderness, she swiftly did what must be done.

▲　▲　▲

They were coming, the men were coming home from the roundup. The screen of dust was on the plain. She had been working on the meal, and now it was the bread she was kneading. Working on the bread, she felt a kick against her abdomen.

She stopped, startled a moment, her hands deep, gripping in the dough—the kick again, strong.

Suddenly, in a way that would have shocked her mother, in a way that would have shocked herself not so long ago, she threw back her head and laughed, a fierce song of love and expectancy. She made bread and was kicked; she expected her man and she laughed, fiercely and tenderly. She was kicked, and a child of the plains had awakened within her. ∾

RESPONDING TO CLUSTER THREE

WHAT WOULD YOU RISK?

Thinking Skill   EVALUATING

1. Choose a main character from the selections in this cluster, and **evaluate** the risks the character takes and the gains, if any, that follow the risk. Do you think that what the character gains is worth the risk? Be prepared to explain your answer. Use a chart such as the one below to start your thinking.

Character	What he/she risked	What he/she gained	Worth the risk?
mother baboon			
the man in the water			
Jared			
Nora			

2. Compare the risks taken in "Plainswoman" by Pleny and Nora. In your opinion, who takes the bigger risk? Be prepared to support your answer with information from the text.

3. Create a brief outline detailing how "Jared," "Plainswoman," or "Battle by the Breadfruit Tree" would be different if the story were told from another character's **point of view.**

4. Say you are given the task of cutting one story from this book. Use your **evaluation** skills to select the story to cut. Be prepared to discuss the criteria, or reasons, you used to make your decision.

Writing Activity: Evaluating Characters

Choose four characters, real or fictional, from this book. Write an evaluation of each character's strengths, weaknesses, and survival skills. Then pick the one character you would want as your partner in a survival situation. Explain your choice.

A Strong Evaluation

- identifies characteristics and criteria
- assesses strong and weak points
- determines value

CLUSTER FOUR

INTO THE WILD

JON KRAKAUER

James Gallien had driven five miles out of Fairbanks when he spotted the hitchhiker standing in the snow beside the road, thumb raised high, shivering in the gray Alaskan dawn. A rifle protruded from the young man's pack, but he looked friendly enough; a hitchhiker with a Remington semiautomatic isn't the sort of thing that gives motorists pause in the 49th state. Gallien steered his four-by-four onto the shoulder and told him to climb in.

The hitchhiker introduced himself as Alex. "Alex?" Gallien responded, fishing for a last name.

"Just Alex," the young man replied, pointedly rejecting the bait. He explained that he wanted a ride as far as the edge of Denali National Park, where he intended to walk deep into the bush and "live off the land for a few months." Alex's backpack appeared to weigh only 25 or 30 pounds, which struck Gallien, an accomplished outdoorsman, as an improbably light load for a three-month sojourn in the backcountry, especially so early in the spring. Immediately Gallien began to wonder if he'd picked up one of those crackpots from the Lower 48 who come north to live out their ill-considered Jack London fantasies.[1] Alaska has long been a magnet for unbalanced souls, often outfitted with little more than innocence and

1 **Jack London fantasies:** author Jack London wrote about life in the wilds of Alaska.

desire, who hope to find their footing in the unsullied enormity of the Last Frontier. The bush, however, is a harsh place and cares nothing for hope or longing. More than a few such dreamers have met predictably unpleasant ends.

As they got to talking during the three-hour drive, though, Alex didn't strike Gallien as your typical misfit. He was congenial, seemed well educated, and peppered Gallien with sensible questions about "what kind of small game lived in the country, what kind of berries he could eat, that kind of thing."

Still, Gallien was concerned: Alex's gear seemed excessively slight for the rugged conditions of the interior bush, which in April still lay buried under the winter snowpack. He admitted that the only food in his pack was a ten-pound bag of rice. He had no compass; the only navigational aid in his possession was a tattered road map he'd scrounged at a gas station, and when they arrived where Alex asked to be dropped off, he left the map in Gallien's truck, along with his watch, his comb, and all his money, which amounted to 85 cents. "I don't want to know what time it is," Alex declared cheerfully. "I don't want to know what day it is, or where I am. None of that matters."

During the drive south toward the mountains, Gallien had tried repeatedly to dissuade[2] Alex from his plan, to no avail. He even offered to drive Alex all the way to Anchorage so he could at least buy the kid some decent gear. "No, thanks anyway," Alex replied. "I'll be fine with what I've got." When Gallien asked whether his parents or some friend knew what he was up to—anyone who could sound the alarm if he got into trouble and was overdue—Alex answered calmly that, no, nobody knew of his plans, that in fact he hadn't spoken to his family in nearly three years. "I'm absolutely positive," he assured Gallien, "I won't run into anything I can't deal with on my own."

"There was just no talking the guy out of it," Gallien recalls. "He was determined. He couldn't wait to head out there and get started." So Gallien drove Alex to the head of the Stampede Trail, an old mining track that begins ten miles west of the town of Healy, convinced him to accept a tuna melt and a pair of rubber boots to keep his feet dry, and wished him good luck. Alex pulled a camera from his backpack and asked Gallien to snap a picture of him. Then, smiling broadly, he disappeared down the snow-covered trail. The date was Tuesday, April 28, 1992.

2 **dissuade:** to advise a person against something.

Chris McCandless, just before he walked into the wild.

More than four months passed before Gallien heard anything more of the hitchhiker. His real name turned out to be Christopher J. McCandless. He was the product of a happy family from an affluent suburb of Washington, D.C. And although he wasn't burdened with a surfeit[3] of common sense and possessed a streak of stubborn idealism that did not readily mesh with the realities of modern life, he was no psychopath. McCandless was in fact an honors graduate of Emory University, an accomplished athlete, and a veteran of several solo excursions into wild, inhospitable terrain.

An extremely intense young man, McCandless had been captivated by the writing of Leo Tolstoy.[4] He particularly admired the fact that the great novelist had forsaken a life of wealth and privilege to wander among the destitute. For several years he had been emulating the count's asceticism[5] and moral rigor to a degree that astonished and occasionally alarmed those who knew him well. When he took leave of James Gallien, McCandless entertained no illusions that he was trekking into Club Med;[6] peril, adversity, and Tolstoyan renunciation were what he was seeking. And that is precisely what he found on the Stampede Trail, in spades.

3 **surfeit:** an overabundant supply.

4 **Leo Tolstoy:** Russian novelist and moral philosopher. He was known as an early champion of nonviolent protest.

5 **asceticism:** practicing self-denial as a measure of personal or spiritual discipline.

6 **Club Med:** a chain of vacation resorts.

For most of 16 weeks McCandless more than held his own. Indeed, were it not for one or two innocent and seemingly insignificant blunders he would have walked out of the Alaskan woods in July or August as anonymously as he walked into them in April. Instead, the name of Chris McCandless has become the stuff of tabloid headlines, and his bewildered family is left clutching the shards of a fierce and painful love.

On the northern margin of the Alaska Range, just before the hulking escarpments of Denali and its satellites surrender to the low Kantishna plain, a series of lesser ridges known as the Outer Ranges sprawls across the flats like a rumpled blanket on an unmade bed. Between the flinty crests of the two outermost Outer Ranges runs an east-west trough, maybe five miles across, carpeted in a boggy amalgam of muskeg, alder thickets, and scrawny spruce. Meandering through this tangled, rolling bottomland is the Stampede Trail, the route Chris McCandless followed into the wilderness.

Twenty or so miles due west of Healy, not far from the boundary of Denali National Park, a derelict bus—a blue and white, 1940s-vintage International from the Fairbanks City Transit System—rusts incongruously[7] in the fireweed beside the Stampede Trail. Many winters ago the bus was fitted with bedding and a crude barrel stove, then skidded into the bush by a road-building crew to serve as a backcountry shelter. These days it isn't unusual for nine or ten months to pass without the bus seeing a human visitor, but on September 6, 1992, six people in three separate parties happened to visit it on the same afternoon, including Ken Thompson, Gordon Samel, and Ferdie Swanson, moose hunters who drove in on all-terrain vehicles.

When they arrived at the bus, says Thompson, they found "a guy and a girl from Anchorage standing 50 feet away, looking kinda spooked. A real bad smell was coming from inside the bus, and there was this weird note tacked by the door." The note, written in neat block letters on a page torn from a novel by Gogol, read: "S.O.S. I need your help. I am injured, near death, and too weak to hike out of here. I am all alone, this is no joke. In the name of God, please remain to save me. I am out collecting berries close by and shall return this evening. Thank you, Chris McCandless. August?"

The Anchorage couple had been too upset by the implications of the note to examine the bus's interior, so Thompson and Samel steeled

---

7 **incongruously:** not conforming; inconsistently.

themselves to take a look. A peek through a window revealed a .22-caliber rifle, a box of shells, some books and clothing, a backpack, and, on a makeshift bunk in the rear of the vehicle, a blue sleeping bag that appeared to have something or someone inside it.

"It was hard to be absolutely sure," says Samel. "I stood on a stump, reached through a back window, and gave the bag a shake. There was definitely something in it, but whatever it was didn't weigh much. It wasn't until I walked around to the other side and saw a head sticking out that I knew for certain what it was." Chris McCandless had been dead for some two and a half weeks.

The Alaska State Troopers were contacted, and the next morning a police helicopter evacuated the decomposed body, a camera with five rolls of exposed film, and a diary—written across the last two pages of a field guide to edible plants—that recorded the young man's final weeks in 113 terse, haunting entries. An autopsy revealed no internal injuries or broken bones. Starvation was suggested as the most probable cause of death. McCandless's signature had been penned at the bottom of the S.O.S. note, and the photos, when developed, included many self-portraits. But because he had been carrying no identification, the police knew almost nothing about who he was or where he was from.

▲   ▲   ▲

Carthage, South Dakota, population 274, is a sleepy little cluster of clapboard houses, weathered brick storefronts, and shaded yards that rises humbly from the immensity of the northern plains, adrift in time. It has one grocery, one bank, a single gas station, a lone bar—the Cabaret, where Wayne Westerberg, a hyperkinetic[8] man with thick shoulders and a rakish black goatee, is sipping a White Russian, chewing on a sweet cigar, and remembering the enigmatic[9] young man he knew as Alex. "These are what Alex used to drink," says Westerberg with a smile, hoisting his glass. "He used to sit right there at the end of the bar and tell us these amazing stories of his travels. He could talk for hours."

Westerberg owns a grain elevator in town but spends every summer running a custom combine crew that follows the harvest from Texas north to Montana. In September 1990 he'd been in Montana cutting barley when, on the highway east of Cut Bank, he'd given a ride to a

---

8 **hyperkinetic:** hyperactive.

9 **enigmatic:** something or someone that is hard to explain or mysterious.

hungry-looking hitchhiker, a friendly young man who said his name was Alex McCandless. They hit it off immediately, and before they went their separate ways Westerberg told Alex to look him up in Carthage if he ever needed a job. "About two weeks later," says Westerberg, "he thumbed into town, moved into my house, and went to work at the elevator. He was the hardest worker I've ever seen. And totally honest—what you'd call extremely ethical. He set pretty high standards for himself.

"You could tell right away that Alex was intelligent," Westerberg continues. "In fact, I think maybe part of what got him into trouble was that he did too much thinking. Sometimes he tried too hard to make sense of the world, to figure out why people were bad to each other so often. A couple of times I tried to tell him it was a mistake to get too deep into that kind of stuff, but Alex got stuck on things. He always had to know the absolute right answer before he could go on to the next thing."

McCandless didn't stay in Carthage long—by the end of October he was on the road again—but he dropped Westerberg a postcard every month or two in the course of his travels. He also had all his mail forwarded to Westerberg's house and told everybody he met thereafter that he was from South Dakota.

In truth McCandless had been raised in the comfortable, upper-middle-class environs of Annandale, Virginia. His father, Walt, was an aerospace engineer who ran a small but very prosperous consulting firm with Chris's mother, Billie. There were eight children in the extended family: Chris; a younger sister, Carine, with whom Chris was extremely close; and six older half-siblings from Walt's first marriage.

McCandless had graduated in June 1990 from Emory University in Atlanta, where he distinguished himself as a history/anthropology major and was offered but declined membership in Phi Beta Kappa, insisting that titles and honors were of no importance. His education had been paid for by a college fund established by his parents; there was some $20,000 in this account at the time of his graduation, money his parents thought he intended to use for law school. Instead, he donated the entire sum to the Oxford Famine Relief Fund. Then, without notifying any friends or family members, he loaded all his belongings into a decrepit yellow Datsun and headed west without itinerary, relieved to shed a life of abstraction and security, a life he felt was removed from the heat and throb of the real world. Chris McCandless intended to invent a new life for himself, one in which he would be free to wallow in unfiltered experience.

In July 1990, on a 120-degree afternoon near Lake Mead, his car broke down and he abandoned it in the Arizona desert. McCandless was exhilarated, so much so that he decided to bury most of his worldly possessions in the parched earth of Detrital Wash and then—in a gesture that would have done Tolstoy proud—burned his last remaining cash, about $160 in small bills. We know this because he documented the conflagration, and most of the events that followed, in a journal/snapshot album he would later give to Westerberg. Although the tone of the journal occasionally veers toward melodrama, the available evidence indicates that McCandless did not misrepresent the facts; telling the truth was a credo he took very seriously.

McCandless tramped around the West for the next two months, spellbound by the scale and power of the landscape, thrilled by minor brushes with the law, savoring the intermittent company of other vagabonds he met along the way. He hopped trains, hitched rides, and walked the trails of the Sierra Nevada before crossing paths with Westerberg in Montana.

In November he sent Westerberg a postcard from Phoenix, urging him to read *War and Peace* ("It has things in it that I think you will understand, things that escape most people") and complaining that thanks to the money Westerberg had paid him, tramping had become too easy. "My days were more exciting when I was penniless and had to forage around for my next meal," he wrote. "I've decided that I'm going to live this life for some time to come. The freedom and simple beauty of it is just too good to pass up. One day I'll get back to you, Wayne, and repay some of your kindness."

Immediately after writing that card, McCandless bought a secondhand aluminum canoe near the head of Lake Havasu and decided to paddle it down the Colorado River all the way to the Gulf of California. En route he sneaked into Mexico by shooting the spillway of a small dam and got lost repeatedly. But he made it to the gulf, where he struggled to control the canoe in a violent squall far from shore and, exhausted, decided to head north again.

On January 16, 1991, McCandless left the stubby metal boat on a hummock of dune grass southeast of Golfo de Santa Clara and started walking north up the deserted beach. He had not seen or talked to another soul in 36 days. For that entire period he had subsisted on nothing but five pounds of rice and what he could pull from the sea, an experience that would later convince him he could survive on similarly meager rations when he went to live in the Alaskan bush. Back at the border two days later, he was caught trying to slip into the United States without ID and spent a night in custody before concocting a story that got him across.

McCandless spent most of the next year in the Southwest, but the last entry in the journal he left with Westerberg is dated May 10, 1991, and so the record of his travels in this period is sketchy. He slummed his way through San Diego, El Paso, and Houston. To avoid being rolled and robbed by the unsavory characters who ruled the streets and freeway overpasses where he slept, he learned to bury what money he had before entering a city, then recover it on the way out of town. Snapshots in the album document visits to Bryce and Zion, the Grand Canyon, Joshua Tree, Palm Springs. For several weeks he lived with "bums, tramps, and winos" on the streets of Las Vegas.

When 1991 drew to a close McCandless was in Bullhead City, Arizona, where for three months he lived in a vacant trailer and flipped burgers at McDonald's. A letter from this period reveals that "a girl Tracy" had a crush on him. In a note to Westerberg he admitted that he liked Bullhead City and "might finally settle down and abandon my tramping life, for good. I'll see what happens when spring comes around, because that's when I tend to get really itchy feet."

Itchy feet prevailed. He soon called Westerberg and said that he wanted to work in the grain elevator for a while, just long enough to put together a little grubstake.[10] He needed money to buy some new gear, he said, because he was going to Alaska.

When McCandless arrived back in Carthage on a bitter February morning in 1992, he'd already decided that he would depart for Alaska on April 15. He wanted to be in Fairbanks by the end of April in order to have as much time as possible in the North before heading back to South Dakota to help out with the autumn harvest. By mid-April Westerberg was shorthanded and very busy, so he asked McCandless to postpone his departure date and work a week or two longer. But, Westerberg says, "Once Alex made up his mind about something there was no changing it. I even offered to buy him a plane ticket to Fairbanks, which would have let him work an extra ten days and still get to Alaska by the end of April. But he said, 'No, I want to hitch north. Flying would be cheating. It would wreck the whole trip.' "

10 **grubstake:** money and supplies saved.

McCandless left Carthage on April 15. In early May Westerberg received a postcard of a polar bear, postmarked April 27. "Greetings from Fairbanks!" it read.

This is the last you shall hear from me Wayne. Arrived here 2 days ago. It was very difficult to catch rides in the Yukon Territory. But I finally got here. Please return all mail I receive to the sender.

It might be a very long time before I return South. If this adventure proves fatal and you don't ever hear from me again, I want you to know your [sic] a great man. I now walk into the wild.

Wayne Westerberg with the postcard he received from McCandless.

McCandless's last postcard to Westerberg fueled widespread speculation, after his adventure did prove fatal, that he'd intended suicide from the start, that when he walked into the bush alone he had no intention of ever walking out again. But I for one am not so sure.

In 1977, when I was 23—a year younger than McCandless at the time of his death—I hitched a ride to Alaska on a fishing boat and set off alone into the backcountry to attempt an ascent of a malevolent stone digit called the Devils Thumb, a towering prong of vertical rock and avalanching ice, ignoring pleas from friends, family, and utter strangers to come to my senses. Simply reaching the foot of the mountain entailed traveling 30 miles up a badly crevassed, storm-wracked glacier that hadn't seen a human footprint in many years. By choice I had no radio, no way of summoning help, no safety net of any kind. I had several harrowing shaves, but eventually I reached the summit of the Thumb.

When I decided to go to Alaska that April, I was an angst-ridden youth who read too much Nietzsche,[11] mistook passion for insight, and func-

11 **Friedrich Nietzsche:** a German philosopher who taught that a being could control his or her passions and therefore use them in a creative manner.

tioned according to an obscure gap-ridden logic. I thought climbing the Devils Thumb would fix all that was wrong with my life. In the end it changed almost nothing, of course. I came to appreciate, however, that mountains make poor receptacles for dreams. And I lived to tell my tale.

As a young man, I was unlike Chris McCandless in many important respects—most notably I lacked his intellect and his altruistic[12] leanings—but I suspect we had a similar intensity, a similar heedlessness, a similar agitation of the soul.

The fact that I survived my Alaskan adventure and McCandless did not survive his was largely a matter of chance; had I died on the Stikine Icecap in 1977 people would have been quick to say of me, as they now say of him, that I had a death wish. Fifteen years after the event, I now recognize that I suffered from hubris, perhaps, and a monstrous innocence, certainly, but I wasn't suicidal.

At the time, death was a concept I understood only in the abstract. I didn't yet appreciate its terrible finality or the havoc it could wreak on those who'd entrusted the deceased with their hearts. I was stirred by the mystery of death; I couldn't resist stealing up to the edge of doom and peering over the brink. The view into that swirling black vortex terrified me, but I caught sight of something elemental in that shadowy glimpse, some forbidden, fascinating riddle.

That's a very different thing from wanting to die.

Westerberg heard nothing else from McCandless for the remainder of the spring and summer. Then, on September 13, 1992, he was rolling down an empty ribbon of South Dakota blacktop, leading his harvest crew home to Carthage after wrapping up a four-month cutting season in northern Montana, when the VHF barked to life. "Wayne!" an anxious voice crackled over the radio from one of the crew's other trucks. "Quick—turn on your AM and listen to Paul Harvey. He's talking about some kid who starved to death up in Alaska. The police don't know who he is. Sounds a whole lot like Alex."

As soon as he got to Carthage, a dispirited Westerberg called the Alaska State Troopers and said that he thought he knew the identity of the hiker. McCandless had never told Westerberg anything about his family, including where they lived, but Westerberg unearthed a W-4 form bearing McCandless's Social Security number, which led the police to an address in Virginia. A few days after the Paul Harvey broadcast, an

---

12 **altruistic:** unselfish regard for the welfare of others.

Alaskan police sergeant made a phone call to the distant suburbs of the nation's capital, confirming the worst fears of Walt and Billie McCandless and raining a flood of confusion and grief down upon their world.

Walt McCandless, 56, dressed in gray sweatpants and a rayon jacket bearing the logo of the Jet Propulsion Laboratory, is a stocky, bearded man with longish salt-and-pepper hair combed straight back from a high forehead. Seven weeks after his youngest son's body turned up in Alaska wrapped in a blue sleeping bag that Billie had sewn for Chris from a kit, he studies a sailboat scudding beneath the window of his waterfront townhouse. "How is it," he wonders aloud as he gazes blankly across Chesapeake Bay, "that a kid with so much compassion could cause his parents so much pain?"

Four large pieces of posterboard covered with dozens of photos documenting the whole brief span of Chris's life stand on the dining room table. Moving deliberately around the display, Billie points out Chris as a toddler astride a hobbyhorse, Chris as a rapt eight-year-old in a yellow slicker on his first backpacking trip, Chris at his high school commencement. "The hardest part," says Walt, pausing over a shot of his son clowning around on a family vacation, "is simply not having him around any more. I spent a lot of time with Chris, perhaps more than with any of my other kids. I really liked his company, even though he frustrated us so often."

It is impossible to know what murky convergence of chromosomal matter, parent-child dynamics, and alignment of the cosmos was responsible, but Chris McCandless came into the world with unusual gifts and a will not easily deflected from its trajectory. As early as third grade, a bemused teacher was moved to pull Chris's parents aside and inform them that their son "marched to a different drummer." At the age of ten, he entered his first running competition, a 10k road race, and finished 69th, beating more than 1,000 adults. By high school he was effortlessly bringing home A's (punctuated by a single F, the result of butting heads with a particularly rigid physics teacher) and had developed into one of the top distance runners in the region.

As captain of his high school cross-country team he concocted novel, grueling training regimens that his teammates still remember well. "Chris invented this workout he called Road Warriors," explains Gordy Cucullu, a close friend from those days. "He would lead us on long, killer runs, as far and as fast as we could go, down strange roads, through the woods, whatever. The whole idea was to lose our bearings, to push ourselves into unknown territory. Then we'd run at a slightly slower pace until we found a road we recognized, and race home again at full speed. In a certain sense, that's how Chris lived his entire life."

McCandless viewed running as an intensely spiritual exercise akin to meditation. "Chris would use the spiritual aspect to try to motivate us," recalls Eric Hathaway, another friend on the team. "He'd tell us to think about all the evil in the world, all the hatred, and imagine ourselves running against the forces of darkness, the evil wall that was trying to keep us from running our best. He believed doing well was all mental, a simple matter of harnessing whatever energy was available. As impressionable high school kids, we were blown away by that kind of talk."

McCandless's musings on good and evil were more than a training technique; he took life's inequities to heart. "Chris didn't understand how people could possibly be allowed to go hungry, especially in this country," says Billie McCandless, a small woman with large, expressive eyes—the same eyes Chris is said to have had. "He would rave about that kind of thing for hours."

For months he spoke seriously of traveling to South Africa and joining the struggle to end apartheid.[13] On weekends, when his high school pals were attending keggers and trying to sneak into Georgetown bars, McCandless would wander the seedier quarters of Washington, chatting with pimps and hookers and homeless people, buying them meals, earnestly suggesting ways they might improve their lives. Once, he actually picked up a homeless man from downtown D.C., brought him to the leafy streets of Annandale, and secretly set him up in the Airstream trailer that his parents kept parked in the driveway. Walt and Billie never even knew they were hosting a vagrant.

McCandless's personality was puzzling in its complexity. He was intensely private but could be convivial and gregarious[14] in the extreme. And despite his overdeveloped social conscience, he was no tight-lipped, perpetually grim do-gooder who frowned on fun. To the contrary, he enjoyed tipping a glass now and then and was an incorrigible ham who would seize any excuse to regale friends and strangers with spirited renditions of Tony Bennett tunes. In college he directed and starred in a witty video parody of Geraldo Rivera opening Al Capone's vault. And he

13 **apartheid:** a South African political system of separating the white and black races.

14 **convivial and gregarious:** liking companionship and fun.

was a natural salesman: Throughout his youth McCandless launched a series of entrepreneurial schemes (a photocopying service, among others), some of which brought in impressive amounts of cash.

Upon graduating from high school, he took the earnings he'd socked away, bought a used Datsun B210, and promptly embarked on the first of his extemporaneous transcontinental odysseys. For half the summer he complied with his parents' insistence that he phone every three days, but he didn't check in at all the last couple of weeks and returned just two days before he was due at college, sporting torn clothes, a scruffy beard, and tangled hair and packing a machete and a .30-06 rifle, which he insisted on taking with him to school.

With each new adventure, Walt and Billie grew increasingly anxious about the risks Chris was taking. Before his senior year at Emory he returned from a summer on the road looking gaunt and weak, having shed 30 pounds from his already lean frame; he'd gotten lost in the Mojave Desert, it turned out, and had nearly succumbed to dehydration. Walt and Billie urged their son to exercise more caution in the future and pleaded with him to keep them better informed of his whereabouts; Chris responded by telling them even less about his escapades and checking in less frequently when he was on the road. "He thought we were idiots for worrying about him," Billie says. "He took pride in his ability to go without food for extended periods, and he had complete confidence that he could get himself out of any jam."

"He was good at almost everything he ever tried," says Walt, "which made him supremely overconfident. If you attempted to talk him out of something, he wouldn't argue. He'd just nod politely and then do exactly what he wanted."

McCandless could be generous and caring to a fault, but he had a darker side as well, characterized by monomania,[15] impatience, and unwavering self-absorption, qualities that seemed to intensify throughout his college years. "I saw Chris at a party after his freshman year at Emory," remembers Eric Hathaway, "and it was obvious that he had changed. He seemed very introverted, almost cold. Social life at Emory revolved around fraternities and sororities, something Chris wanted no part of. And when everybody started going Greek,[16] he kind of pulled back from his old friends and got more heavily into himself."

---

15 **monomania:** excessive concentration on one thought or idea.
16 **going Greek:** joining a fraternity or sorority.

When Walt and Billie went to Atlanta in the spring of 1990 for Chris's college graduation, he told them that he was planning another summer-long trip and that he'd drive up to visit them in Annandale before hitting the road. But he never showed. Shortly thereafter he donated the $20,000 in his bank account to Oxfam, loaded up his car, and disappeared. From then on he scrupulously avoided contacting either his parents or Carine, the sister for whom he purportedly cared immensely.

"We were all worried when we didn't hear from him," says Carine, "and I think my parents' worry was mixed with hurt and anger. But I didn't really feel hurt. I knew that he was happy and doing what he wanted to do. I understood that it was important for him to see how independent he could be. And he knew that if he wrote or called me, Mom and Dad would find out where he was, fly out there, and try to bring him home."

In September—by which time Chris had long since abandoned the yellow Datsun in the desert and burned his money—Walt and Billie grew worried enough to hire a private investigator. "We worked pretty hard to trace him," says Walt. "We eventually picked up his trail on the northern California coast, where he'd gotten a ticket for hitchhiking, but we lost track of him for good right after that, probably about the time he met Wayne Westerberg." Walt and Billie would hear nothing more about Chris's whereabouts until their son's body turned up in Alaska two years later.

After Chris had been identified, Carine and their oldest half-brother, Sam, flew to Fairbanks to bring home his ashes and those few possessions—the rifle, a fishing rod, a Swiss Army knife, the book in which he'd kept his journal, and not much else—that had been recovered with the body, including the photographs he'd taken in Alaska. Sifting through this pictorial record of Chris's final days, it is all Billie can do to force herself to examine the fuzzy snapshots. As she studies the pictures she breaks down from time to time, weeping as only a mother who has outlived a child can weep, betraying a sense of loss so huge and irreparable that the mind balks at taking its measure. Such bereavement, witnessed at close range, makes even the most eloquent apologia for high-risk activities ring fatuous and hollow.

"I just don't understand why he had to take those kinds of chances," Billie protests through her tears. "I just don't understand it at all."

When news of McCandless's fate came to light, most Alaskans were quick to dismiss him as a nut case. According to the conventional wisdom he was simply one more dreamy, half-cocked greenhorn who went into the bush expecting to find answers to all his problems and instead found nothing but mosquitoes and a lonely death.

Dozens of marginal characters have gone into the Alaskan backcountry over the years, never to reappear. A few have lodged firmly in the state's collective memory. There is, for example, the sad tale of John Mallon Waterman, a visionary climber much celebrated for making one of the most astonishing first ascents in the history of North American mountaineering—an extremely dangerous 145-day solo climb of Mount Hunter's Southeast Spur. Upon completing this epic deed in 1979, though, he found that instead of putting his demons to rest, success merely agitated them.

In the years that followed, Waterman's mind unraveled. He took to prancing around Fairbanks in a black cape and announced he was running for president under the banner of the Feed the Starving Party, the main priority of which was to ensure that nobody on the planet died of hunger. To publicize his campaign he laid plans to make a solo ascent of Denali, in winter, with a minimum of food.

After his first attempt on the mountain was aborted prematurely, Waterman committed himself to the Anchorage Psychiatric Institute but checked out after two weeks, convinced that there was a conspiracy afoot to put him away permanently. Then, in the winter of 1981, he launched another solo attempt on Denali. He was last placed on the upper Ruth Glacier, heading unroped through the middle of a deadly crevasse field[17] en route to the mountain's difficult East Buttress, carrying neither sleeping bag nor tent. He was never seen after that, but a note was later found atop some of his gear in a nearby shelter. It read, "3-13-81 My last kiss 1:42 PM."

Perhaps inevitably, parallels have been drawn between John Waterman and Chris McCandless. Comparisons have also been made between McCandless and Carl McCunn, a likable, absentminded Texan who in 1981 paid a bush pilot to drop him at a lake deep in the Brooks Range to photograph wildlife. He flew in with 500 rolls of film and 1,400 pounds of provisions but forgot to arrange for the pilot to pick him up again. Nobody realized he was missing until state troopers came across his body a year later, lying beside a 100-page diary that documented his demise. Rather than starve, McCunn had reclined in his tent and shot himself in the head.

17 **crevasse field:** area with many steep cracks.

There are similarities among Waterman, McCunn, and McCandless, most notably a certain dreaminess and a paucity[18] of common sense. But unlike Waterman, McCandless was not mentally unbalanced. And unlike McCunn, he didn't go into the bush assuming that someone would magically appear to bring him out again before he came to grief.

McCandless doesn't really conform to the common bush-casualty stereotype: He wasn't a kook, he wasn't an outcast, and although he was rash and incautious to the point of foolhardiness, he was hardly incompetent or he would never have lasted 113 days. If one is searching for predecessors cut from the same exotic cloth, if one hopes to understand the personal tragedy of Chris McCandless by placing it in some larger context, one would do well to look at another northern land, in a different century altogether.

Off the southeastern coast of Iceland sits a low barrier island called Papos. Treeless and rocky, perpetually knocked by gales howling off the North Atlantic, the island takes its name from its first settlers, now long gone, the Irish monks known as papar. They arrived as early as the fifth and sixth centuries A.D., having sailed and rowed from the western coast of Ireland. Setting out in small open boats called curraghs, made from cowhide stretched over light wicker frames, they crossed one of the most treacherous stretches of ocean in the world without knowing what they'd find on the other side.

The papar risked their lives—and lost them in untold droves—but not in the pursuit of wealth or personal glory or to claim new lands in the name of a despot.[19] As the great Arctic explorer Fridtjof Nansen points out, they undertook their remarkable voyages "chiefly from the wish to find lonely places, where these anchorites[20] might dwell in peace, undisturbed by the turmoil and temptations of the world." When the first handful of Norwegians showed up on the shores of Iceland in the ninth century, the papar decided the country had become too crowded, even though it was still all but uninhabited. They climbed back into into their curraghs and rowed off toward Greenland. They were drawn west across the storm-wracked ocean, past the edge of the known world, by nothing more than hunger of the spirit, a queer, pure yearning that burned in their souls.

18 **paucity:** lack.
19 **despot:** absolute ruler of a country.
20 **anchorites:** hermits.

Reading of these monks, one is struck by their courage, their reckless innocence, and the intensity of their desire. And one can't help thinking of Chris McCandless.

On April 25, 1992, ten days after leaving South Dakota, McCandless rode his thumb into Fairbanks. After perusing the classified ads, he bought a used Remington Nylon 66—a semiautomatic .22-caliber rifle with a 4x20 scope and a plastic stock that was favored by Alaskan trappers for its light weight and reliability.

One of the photos Chris took of himself.

When James Gallien dropped McCandless off at the head of the Stampede Trail on April 28 the temperature was in the low thirties—it would drop into the low teens at night—and a foot of crusty spring snow covered the ground. As he trudged expectantly down the trail in a fake-fur parka, the heaviest item in McCandless's half-full backpack was his library: nine or ten paperbacks ranging from Michael Crichton's *The Terminal Man* to Thoreau's *Walden* and Tolstoy's *The Death of Ivan Illyich*. One of these volumes, *Tanaina Plantlore,* by Priscilla Russel Kari, was a scholarly, exhaustively researched field guide to edible plants in the region; it was in the back of this book that McCandless began keeping an abbreviated record of his journey.

From his journal we know that on April 29 McCandless fell through the ice—perhaps crossing the frozen surface of the Teklanika River, perhaps in the maze of broad, shallow beaver ponds that lie just beyond its western bank—although there is no indication that he suffered any injury. A day later he got his first glimpse of Denali's gleaming white ramparts, and a day after that, about 20 miles down the trail from where he started, he stumbled upon the bus and decided to make it his base camp.

He was elated to be there. Inside the bus, on a sheet of weathered plywood spanning a broken window, McCandless scrawled an exultant declaration of independence:

Two years he walks the earth. No phone, no pool, no pets, no cigarettes.
Ultimate freedom. An extremist. An aesthetic voyager whose home is the
road. Escaped from Atlanta. Thou shalt not return, 'cause "the West is
the best." And now after two rambling years comes the final and greatest
adventure. The climactic battle to kill the false being within and victoriously
conclude the spiritual pilgrimage. Ten days and nights of freight trains
and hitchhiking bring him to the Great White North. No longer to be
poisoned by civilization he flees, and walks alone upon the land to
become lost in the wild.

Alexander Supertramp
May 1992

But reality quickly intruded. McCandless had difficulty killing game, and the daily journal entries during his first week at the bus include "weakness," "snowed in," and "disaster." He saw but did not shoot a grizzly on May 2, shot at but missed some ducks on May 4, and finally killed and ate a spruce grouse on May 5. But he didn't kill any more game until May 9, when he bagged a single small squirrel, by which point he'd written "4th day famine" in the journal.

Soon thereafter McCandless's fortunes took a sharp turn for the better. By mid-May the snowpack was melting down to bare ground, exposing the previous season's rose hips and lingonberries, preserved beneath the frost, which he gathered and ate. He also became much more successful at hunting and for the next six weeks feasted regularly on squirrel, spruce grouse, duck, goose, and porcupine. On May 22 he lost a crown from a tooth, but it didn't seem to dampen his spirits much, because the following day he scrambled up the nameless 3,000-foot butte that rose directly north of the bus, giving him a view of the whole icy sweep of the Alaska Range and mile after mile of stunning, completely uninhabited country. His journal entry for the day is characteristically terse but unmistakably joyous: "CLIMB MOUNTAIN!"

Although McCandless was enough of a realist to know that hunting was an unavoidable component of living off the land, he had always been ambivalent about killing animals. That ambivalence turned to regret on June 9, when he shot and killed a small female moose. For six days he toiled to preserve the meat, believing that it was morally indefensible to waste any part of an animal that has been killed for food. He butchered the carcass under a thick cloud of flies and mosquitoes, boiled the internal organs into a stew, and then laboriously dug a cave in the rocky earth in which he tried to preserve, by smoking, the huge amount of meat that he was unable to eat immediately. Despite his efforts, on June 14 his journal records, "Maggots already! Smoking appears ineffective. Don't know, looks like disaster. I now wish I had never shot the moose. One of the greatest tragedies of my life."

Although he recriminated himself severely for this waste of a life he had taken, a day later McCandless appeared to regain some perspective—his journal notes, "henceforth will learn to accept my errors, however great they be"—and the period of contentment that began in mid-May resumed and continued until early July. Then, in the midst of this idyll, came the first of two pivotal setbacks.

Satisfied, apparently, with what he had accomplished during his two months of solitary existence, McCandless decided to return to civilization. It was time to bring his "final and greatest adventure" to a close and get himself back to the world of men and women, where he could chug a beer, discuss philosophy, enthrall strangers with tales of what he'd done. He seemed to have turned the corner on his need to assert his autonomy from his parents. He seemed ready, perhaps, to go home. On a parchmentlike strip of birch bark he drew up a list of tasks to do before he departed: "patch jeans, shave!, organize pack." Then, on July 3—the day after a journal entry that reads, "Family happiness"—he shouldered his backpack, departed the bus, and began the 30-mile walk to the highway.

Two days later, halfway to the road, he arrived in heavy rain on the west bank of the Teklanika River, a major stream spawned by distant glaciers on the crest of the Alaska Range. Sixty-seven days earlier it had been frozen over, and he had simply strolled across it. Now, however, swollen with rain and melting snow, the Teklanika was running big, cold, and fast.

If he could reach the far shore, the rest of the hike to the highway would be trivial, but to get there he would have to negotiate a 75-foot channel of chest-deep water that churned with the power of a freight train. In his journal McCandless wrote, "Rained in. River look impossible. Lonely, scared." Concluding that he would drown if he attempted to cross, he turned around and walked back toward the bus, back into the fickle heart of the bush.

McCandless got back to the bus on July 8. It's impossible to know what was going through his mind at that point, believing that his escape had been cut off, for his journal betrays nothing. Actually, he wasn't cut off at all: A quarter-mile downstream from where he had tried to cross, the Teklanika rushes through a narrow gorge spanned by a hand-operated tram—a metal basket suspended from pulleys on a steel cable. If he had known about it, crossing the Teklanika to safety would have been little more than a casual task. Also, six miles due south of the bus, an easy day's walk up the main fork of the Sushana, the National Park Service maintains a cabin stocked with food, bedding, and first-aid supplies for the use of backcountry rangers on their winter patrols. This cabin is plainly marked on most topographic maps of the area, but McCandless, lacking such a map, had no way of knowing about it. His friends point out, of course, that had he carried a map and known the cabin was so close, his muleheaded obsession with self-reliance would have kept him from staying anywhere near the bus; rather, he would have headed even deeper into the bush.

So he went back to the bus, which was a sensible course of action: It was the height of summer, the country was fecund with plant and animal life, and his food supply was still adequate. He probably surmised that if he could just bide his time until August, the Teklanika would subside enough to be forded.

For the rest of July McCandless fell back into his routine of hunting and gathering. His snapshots and journal entries indicate that over those three weeks he killed 35 squirrels, four spruce grouse, five jays and woodpeckers, and two frogs, which he supplemented with wild potatoes, wild rhubarb, various berries, and mushrooms. Despite this apparent munificence, the meat he'd been killing was very lean, and he was consuming fewer calories than he was burning. After three months on a marginal diet, McCandless had run up a sizable caloric deficit. He was balanced on a precarious, razor-thin edge. And then, on July 30, he made the mistake that pulled him down.

His journal entry for that date reads, "Extremely weak. Fault of pot[ato] seed. Much trouble just to stand up. Starving. Great Jeopardy." McCandless had been digging and eating the root of the wild potato—*Hedysarum alpinum,* a common area wildflower also known as Eskimo potato, which Kari's book told him was widely eaten by native Alaskans—for more than a month without ill effect. On July 14 he apparently started eating the pealike seedpods of the plant as well, and the available evidence suggests that these seeds might have slowly, insidiously, poisoned him.

Laid low by the toxic seeds, he was too weak to hunt effectively and thus slid toward starvation. Things began to spin out of control with terrible speed. "DAY 100! MADE IT!" he noted jubilantly on August 5, proud of achieving such a significant milestone, "but in weakest condition of life. Death looms as serious threat. Too weak to walk out."

Over the next week or so the only game he bagged was five squirrels and a spruce grouse. Many Alaskans have wondered why, at this point, he didn't start a forest fire as a distress signal; small planes fly over the area every few days, they say, and the Park Service would surely have dispatched a crew to control the conflagration. "Chris would never intentionally burn down a forest, not even to save his life," answers Carine McCandless. "Anybody who would suggest otherwise doesn't understand the first thing about my brother."

Starvation is not a pleasant way to die. In advanced stages, as the body begins to consume itself, the victim suffers muscle pain, heart disturbances, loss of hair, shortness of breath. Convulsions and hallucinations are not uncommon. Some who have been brought back from the far edge of starvation, though, report that near the end their suffering was replaced by a sublime euphoria, a sense of calm accompanied by transcendent mental clarity. Perhaps, it would be nice to think, McCandless enjoyed a similar rapture.

From August 13 through 18 his journal records nothing beyond a tally of the days. At some point during this week, he tore the final page from Louis L'Amour's memoir, *Education of a Wandering Man*. On one side were some lines that L'Amour had quoted from Robinson Jeffers's poem "Wise Men in Their Bad Hours":

> Death's a fierce meadowlark: but to die having made
> Something more equal to the centuries
> Than muscle and bone, is mostly to shed weakness.

On the other side of the page, which was blank, McCandless penned a brief adios: "I have had a happy life and thank the Lord. Goodbye and may God bless all!"

Then he crawled into the sleeping bag his mother had made for him and slipped into unconsciousness. He probably died on August 18, 113 days after he'd walked into the wild, 19 days before six hunters and hikers would happen across the bus and discover his body inside.

One of his last acts was to take a photograph of himself, standing near the bus under the high Alaskan sky, one hand holding his final note toward the camera lens, the other raised in a brave, beatific[21] farewell. He is smiling in the photo, and there is no mistaking the look in his eyes: Chris McCandless was at peace, serene as a monk gone to God. ∾

21 **beatific:** having a blissful appearance.

This account is an adaptation of an article titled "Death of an Innocent," published in the January 1993 issue of Outside *magazine. A much more complete account of Chris McCandless's remarkable life can be found in Jon Krakauer's best-selling book, INTO THE WILD, published by Anchor Books.*

RESPONDING TO CLUSTER FOUR

ESSENTIAL QUESTION:
WHAT CAN BE LEARNED FROM SURVIVAL LITERATURE?

Thinking Skill SYNTHESIZING

The last selection in this book provides an opportunity for independent learning and the application of the critical thinking skill, synthesis. *Synthesizing* means examining all the things you have learned from this book and combining them to form a richer and more meaningful view of risk-taking and the will to survive.

There are many ways to demonstrate what you know about survival. Here are some possibilities. Your teacher may provide others.

1. Break into small groups, with each group taking responsibility for teaching a part of the final cluster. To teach the lesson you might:

   a) create discussion questions and lead a discussion

   b) develop vocabulary activities

   c) prepare a test for the cluster selections

   As you develop your activity, keep the essential question in mind:
   "What can be learned from survival literature?"

2. It is often said that one reason young people take risks is because they feel invincible—they don't believe death can touch them. Evaluate one of the selections, such as "Into the Wild," and see if that statement applies to the main character.

3. Individually or in small groups, develop an independent project that demonstrates survival skills. For example, you might give a presentation on the training and qualities NASA requires in its astronauts. Other options might include a music video, dance, poem, performance, drama, or artistic rendering.

ACKNOWLEDGMENTS

Text Credits CONTINUED FROM PAGE 2 "Done With," from *The Descent* by Ann Stanford. Copyright © 1970 by Ann Stanford. Used by permission of Viking Penguin, a division of Penguin Putnam Inc.

"Into the Wild," adapted from an article entitled "Death of an Innocent" by Jon Krakauer, *Outside Magazine*, January 1993. Reprinted with permission of the author. A portion of the permission fee has been donated to The Chris McCandless Memorial Fund, P.O. Box 1510, Chesapeake Beach, MD 20732.

"Jared" by David Gifaldi. Reprinted with the permission of Atheneum Books for Young Readers, an imprint of Simon & Schuster Children's Publishing Division from *Rearranging and Other Stories* by David Gifaldi. Copyright © 1998 David Gifaldi.

"The Man in the Water" by Roger Rosenblatt. From the January 25, 1982 issue of *Time Magazine*. Copyright © 1982 Time Inc. Reprinted by permission.

"Plainswoman" by Williams Forrest. First printed in *The Saturday Evening Post*, September 24, 1960. Reprinted by permission of Elaine Forrest.

"Search and Rescue" from *Pass the Butterworms: Remote Journeys Oddly Rendered* by Tim Cahill. Copyright © 1997 by Tim Cahill. Reprinted by permission of Villard Books, a division of Random House, Inc.

"Staying Alive" by David Wagoner. From *Traveling Light: Collected and New Poems, 1957-1998*. Copyright © 1999 by David Wagoner. Used with permission of the University of Illinois Press.

"Wilding" by Jane Yolen. Copyright © 1995 by Jane Yolen. First published by Harcourt Brace in *A Starfarer's Dozen*, Michael Stearns, ed. Reprinted by permission of Curtis Brown, Ltd.

Excerpts from *Winterdance*, copyright © 1994 by Gary Paulsen, reprinted by permission of Harcourt, Inc.

Every reasonable effort has been made to properly acknowledge ownership of all material used. Any omissions or mistakes are not intentional and, if brought to the publisher's attention, will be corrected in future editions.

Photo and Art Credits Cover and Title Page: David Blackwood, *Fire Down on the Labrador*, 1980. Etching 80 x 50.5 cm. Pages 3, 4-5 © Olivia Parker. *At the Edge of the Garden*, 1986. Page 8: (right) © Allan Davey/Masterfile, (left) Owen Franken/CORBIS. Page 9: NASA/CORBIS. Page 11: © Galen Rowell/Peter Arnold, Inc. Page 12: Wanda Wulz, *Me + Cat*, ca. 1932, Alinari/Art Resource, NY. Page 19: Robert Bourdeau, *Costa Rica*, 1989. Courtesy Jane Corkin Gallery, Toronto. Page 25: © 1994 Jeff Schultz/Alaska Stock. Page 29: © 1996 Jeff Schultz/Alaska Stock. Pages 30-31: Ansel Adams Publishing Rights Trust/CORBIS. Page 32: © Kim Heacox/Peter Arnold, Inc. Pages 36-37: © Clint Clemens/International Stock Photography. Page 39: © Doug Lee/Peter Arnold, Inc. Page 40: Carolyn Brady, *Emerald Light (Black Desk for Zola)*, 1984. Watercolor on paper, 60 x 40 in. Courtesy Nancy Hoffman Gallery, NY. Page 47: George Tooker, *Cornice*, ca. 1949. Tempera. Courtesy Columbus Museum of Art, Ohio. Museum Purchase: Howald Fund II. Page 58: © 1997 Marion Stirrup/Alaska Stock. Page 59: © Kim Heacox/Peter Arnold, Inc. Page 65: © 1997 John Warden/Alaska Stock. Page 68: Tom Benoit/© Tony Stone Images. Pages 71: © Clyde H. Smith/Peter Arnold, Inc. Page 73: Index Stock Imagery. Page 74: © BIOS (M & C Denis-Huot)/Peter Arnold, Inc. Pages 80-81: John Dominis/*Life* Magazine, © Time Inc. Page 83: Marvin E. Newman/The Image Bank. Page 84: © Sygma. Page 88: Roloff Beny, *Bronze Youth*, (Detail), National Archives of Canada. Pages 108-109: Courtesy Montana Historical Society, Helena. Page 115: Nebraska Historical Society. Page 119: © Clyde H. Smith/Peter Arnold, Inc. Page 120: Phil Schofield/*PEOPLE Weekly*, © 1992. Pages 123, 137, 142: Courtesy McCandless family. Page 129: Courtesy Jon Krakauer.